THE SEAM ALLOWANCE

THE SEAM ALLOWANCE

Industrial Home Sewing in Canada

by

LAURA C. JOHNSON

with

ROBERT E. JOHNSON

The
Women's
·Press·

CANADIAN CATALOGUING IN PUBLICATION DATA

Johnson, Laura Climenko, 1943-
The seam allowance

Bibliography: p.
ISBN 0-88961-072-X

1. Home labor – Canada. 2. Women – Employment – Canada.
3. Machine sewing – Economic aspects.
I. Johnson, Robert E. II. Title.
HD6073.C62C36   331.4'887   C82-094396-7

Cover photograph by Anna Fraser

Cover and book design by Liz Martin

Printed and bound in Canada
Lithographed by union labour at
Alger Press Ltd., Oshawa, Ontario

Published by the Women's Educational Press
16 Baldwin Street
Toronto, Ontario, Canada

To the memory of Gladys Dickason

PHOTOGRAPHY CREDITS

CONTENTS

PREFACE

Forty years ago, North American trade unionists believed that the system of industrial homework in the garment industry — with its exploitative conditions, long hours and low wages — had finally been laid to rest. In the United States, a formal ban had been instituted on the most common forms of homework. In Canada, homework was subject to various provincial regulations that were intended to protect homeworkers from unfair employment practices. In both countries the number of homeworkers was shrinking from year to year, and it seemed only a matter of time until the homework system would disappear altogether.

And yet, homework still flourishes in the 1980s. In the United States, efforts are underway to remove the forty-year-old ban on homework in the garment industry. In Canada, a number of garment manufacturers have recently switched their operations from factories to a homework system. Changes taking place in microtechnology, moreover, are expected to give rise to revolutionary new forms of "electronic cottage industry." The technology exists to move many of the clerical jobs now done in offices to the home setting.

Clearly, the reports of homework's demise were premature. It exists today for the same reasons that supported it 50 and even 150 years ago. For workers — mainly women with young children — it is a way of combining household commitments with paid employment. For employers it is a way of reducing overhead and keeping wages down.

As a sociologist at the Social Planning Council of Metropolitan Toronto, I became acquainted with the practice of homework in connection with a study of children's day care. The research involved door-to-door interviews with a random sample of Toronto parents, and posed questions about day care arrangements made by working mothers. I discovered that for many immigrant mothers of young children, working means spending long hours sewing at home, simultaneously caring for their children. As one woman said,

Sure I work — I sit in my basement and sew wedding gowns for $7 a piece. What do I do for day care? I take care of my children myself — that's why I'm working in my home.

Through interviews with fifty women who work at home doing industrial sewing and with others involved in the homework system, this book documents the substandard working conditions of homeworkers and attempts to assess the scale of work-at-home in the clothing industry in Canada.

ACKNOWLEDGEMENTS

Homework is part of what is known as the "underground economy." It is an elusive, often highly secretive phenomenon. It is always difficult to commit such an activity to study, and this project would have been impossible without the cooperation of a great number of people. I am very grateful to those who generously donated time and effort and, in a number of cases, took considerable risks. Some must, of necessity, remain nameless and thanks are therefore extended to those people who cared enough about the injustices associated with homework to assist me in my efforts to subject the practice to public scrutiny.

This book is based on interviews with fifty women who work at home doing industrial sewing. Interviews lasting between one and two hours were conducted in the language spoken by the homeworker — Italian, Chinese, Greek — or on a few occasions, French or English. The interviews dealt with rates of pay, conditions of employment, the women's attitudes towards their work and their family backgrounds. When the women gave permission, we took photographs of their work environment. Many of the women were vehement in their denunciation of the unfair labour practices associated with the homework system. A number were unwilling to be photographed because they were afraid that employers would identify them as troublemakers and would withhold work from them.

The reception we received varied considerably from interview to interview. In some cases, the respondents were immediately warm and welcoming. In others, the women were mistrustful of our motives, nervous about our promises of confidentiality and therefore guarded and hurried in their responses. On one occasion, a woman's husband arrived home partway through the interview and insisted that we leave immediately. In another instance, a woman's sister came by during the interview; she was highly suspicious and demanded that the interview be terminated.

In addition to the interviews with women who do homework, this book is also based on interviews with other people familiar with the workings of the homework system — including government officials, trade union officials and employers. These interviews sought to examine the extent of homework in Canada, as well as the existing provisions for regulation and enforcement of employment standards for homeworkers.

My first expression of gratitude goes to the homeworkers themselves. These women, in Toronto, elsewhere in southern Ontario and in Montreal, donated a great deal of their time — a precious commodity in their overworked schedules — to describe the conditions of their employment. Their assistance is gratefully acknowledged.

Most of the interviews were conducted by a team of three women — generally an interpreter, a photographer and myself. The questionnaires contained sensitive and detailed questions, and the interviews demanded considerable skill on the part of the interpreters. Thanks are therefore extended to Annamaria Menozzi, Koula Christodoulou, Selina Man and the other interpreters who assisted with this work.

The photographs in this book comprise an integral part of the description of the homework system. Elizabeth Wilcox, who contributed most of the contemporary photographs, developed an excellent rapport with the homeworkers, putting them at ease as she photographed them. Anna Fraser, who helped to develop the idea for this project, also contributed some of the photographs, and demonstrated a similar ability to create an informal, relaxed setting.

Rona Moreau, who during the study was a student in the Department of Sociology at the University of Toronto, assumed complete responsibility for the gathering of information on homework in Montreal. She conducted extensive interviews with government and union officials in that city, as well as with various people working in the field of services for immigrant women. In addition, she spent several days interviewing Montreal homeworkers. Over the past two years, Rona has worked with me as a research partner in this study, sharing her insights and offering valuable advice on the research design. I greatly appreciate her assistance.

Audrey Ho, a student at the University of Toronto Law School, prepared a review of homework legislation. Under a program funded by the Women's Bureau of the Ontario Ministry of Labour, Audrey worked at the Social Planning Council from May through August 1981. During that time she conducted a comprehensive study of the regulation of homework in a variety of jurisdictions. The information she collected is an important part of this research.

The research for this book was made possible through financial support from the Canadian Research Institute for the Advancement of Women. In addition to providing a research grant-in-aid, the Toronto chapter of CRIAW and numerous individual members offered considerable interest in and support for the research endeavour. That support is gratefully acknowledged. I would also like to credit the Labour Temple, the International Ladies Garment Workers' Union, and the Amalgamated Clothing and Textile Workers' Unions, in Toronto, for grants to assist the publication of this work.

During the three years of this project, countless friends and co-workers have offered advice, suggestions and many different kinds of help. A final word of thanks is due to The Women's Press, and in particular to Meg Luxton and Jane Springer. Meg offered valuable guidance and direction from the earliest stages in the development of the book. Jane edited the manuscript with keen interest and care. In both cases, their assistance went far beyond technical editorial skills; their encouragement has been a major factor in helping to bring this project to fruition.

1

THE HIGH PRICE

OF FASHION

Angelo Lo sews at home. She has two young children, aged three and five. She is married to a restaurant cook. The Lo family lives in a small two-bedroom apartment in a highrise, but they have hopes of moving into a house of their own.

There is no extra room in their apartment, so Angela sews in a closet that she and her husband have adapted for the purpose. She works under an overhead lamp. Her sewing produces a high level of fabric dust and lint in the small, enclosed space.

The dresses Angela Lo sews require a lot of fine detail, and fabric patterns must be matched perfectly. It usually takes her between 45 minutes and an hour to complete a dress. At the rate of $2 to $2.50 for each garment, she is able to earn up to $150 in a good week.

Some months there is lots of work, enough to keep her busy six or even seven days a week, for as much as eight to ten hours of sewing a day. In other months, usually in mid-winter, there is no work. Last year, Angela Lo earned a total of $4,000.

Angela's husband uses the family car to do all of the pick-up and delivery of bundles of garments to and from a factory. Although it would be cheaper to go by public transportation, the bundles are heavy and bulky and one person would not be able to carry them. Besides, the round trip is about ten miles.

❧

Angela Lo in Toronto, together with thousands of her counterparts elsewhere across Canada, make up the vast, hidden homework labour force. All of them women, most of them immigrants, homeworkers produce a remarkable share of the clothing manufactured in Canada. Homeworkers also work on uniforms, linens, toys and other articles produced in the highly labour-intensive needle trades industries.

Also termed "outside workers," homeworkers take work from factories, to be completed in their own homes, using their own machinery and equipment, and paying for their own utilities. These workers lack the protection of trade unions and (for the most part), employment standards legislation. As a result, they often work extended hours at subminimum wages, and receive no benefits. Homeworkers and their families are exposed to numerous health and safety risks as a result of the work they do. Totally isolated from the inside workers who work for the same employers, and from other outside workers, these women have no opportunity to organize to improve the conditions of their employment.

❧

Seven years ago, James Morris owned a clothing factory in Toronto. The enormous increase in imported clothing affected his business and he began losing money. He laid off all but one of his 45 workers — a skilled cutter — and started over again, this time without the factory. He began to take bundles of ready-cut cloth to the women who used to sew for him in the factory. They sewed up the dresses and returned them to him for finishing and pressing. Today, Morris runs a highly successful, moderately-sized dress manufacturing business. Says Morris:

Homework is the only way to go in Canada . . . I won't replace homeworkers for a long time. I don't want another factory.

Morris' workplace now employs only ten workers, who do the cutting, samples, finishing, pressing and office work. He also uses three contractors who have their own factories and/or homeworkers. Morris does not concern himself with the employment conditions of the women who make up his dresses; he cares only that the finished product is made to his exacting specifications and delivered to him in the time agreed. James Morris finds that the homework system meets his needs.

❧

The garment industry is the largest employer of homeworkers in Canada. A $3 billion industry, it accounts for over six per cent of all manufacturing employment in the country — and the figure rises to 25 per cent in some regions.[1] The principal branches of the Canadian industry are men's, women's and children's clothing; fur goods; foundation garments; gloves, hats and caps; hosiery and knitwear. The two largest branches of the industry are men's and women's clothing.

Although there are garment firms all across Canada, the industry is concentrated in the provinces of Quebec, Ontario and Manitoba. According to Statistics Canada, there were 2,318 garment manufacturing firms in Canada in 1975. The regional distribution of these manufacturing establishments is as follows:

Quebec	69.5 per cent
Ontario	21.7 per cent
Manitoba	4.3 per cent
Other provinces	4.5 per cent

Three-quarters of the production in the industry is carried out in urban areas, mainly Montreal, Toronto and Winnipeg.

Total recorded employment in the garment industry is approximately 120,000. On its show February 2, 1982, the Canadian Broadcasting Corporation's investigative TV program, The Fifth Estate, claimed that the number of homeworkers in Canada (largely unrecorded, as we shall see) may be as high as 100,000. The industry employs 75 per cent women, making it the single largest employer of women among manufacturing industries in Canada.[2] Immigrant women comprise a large portion of the workforce in Canada's garment industry. A report prepared by Sheila Arnopoulos for the Canadian Advisory Council on the Status of Women states that, according to the Canada Employment and Immigration Commission, "about half of textile and almost all the clothing industry workers are immigrant women."[3]

❧

Mary Chow's small clothing factory is housed in several rooms in an old loft in Toronto's garment district. Mary Chow is one of the three contractors who make up the garments for James Morris. She also makes up orders for several other apparel firms. She is proud of her small factory, and of the fact that she has worked her way up in Canada's highly competitive garment business.

Mary Chow has been working in the clothing industry in Canada for almost 15 years. She recalls,

> I used to work in a dress factory, but because my kids were born and there was no one to look after the two of them, I began to take homework, first making leather jackets and then evening dresses. When I started as a homeworker, I wasn't very experienced, and I didn't even earn the minimum wage. I sewed constantly, but the garments I sewed didn't bring in much money. We Chinese are hard workers, willing to work over ten hours a day. By working so long hours, I made more money.
>
> When the kids became older and started school, then I started this business of my own. I want to create the styles and sell them directly to the stores. That will be two or three more years, at least.

The number of workers in Mary Chow's factory varies according to her workload. On average, though, she has about 15 sewing machine operators. All of her workers are Chinese and most of them work a seven-day week. According to Mary Chow,

> The operators do not mind working seven days. They are usually quite willing to help out. We are like friends, and not boss-employee.

At present, Mary Chow is using one homeworker, and only for certain specialized tasks, like turning collars and making pleats. These jobs are simple, but they take time. The homeworker is a relative of one of the inside workers at Mary Chow's factory.

In the few short years that she has been a contractor, Mary Chow has lost the perspective of the employee and has appropriated the management view. She is not aware of Ontario's law requiring employers of homeworkers to obtain a permit from the provincial government. Like many other Canadian clothing manufacturers and contractors, Mary Chow is an illegal employer of homeworkers.

Only rarely does Mary Chow use homeworkers, because, she says, her business is not large enough to make it feasible.

If you are big enough, you can save a lot of money using homeworkers. With in-factory work, the overhead is high and I have to pay for rent, hydro and workers even if there's no work. With homeworkers, when you are very busy, you can give them more to do because they don't mind how many hours they do. They also don't mind if there's less to do sometimes. They don't need to be laid off.

But I don't have the manpower to use homeworkers. If you have homeworkers, you have to watch them and you have to make many runs to deliver and pick up the goods. You may have an order of several hundred dresses to make, with many homeworkers making the same style, and they may not all turn out the same. It just takes too much time to control quality. Inside the factory, I can supervise all the work myself.

❧

Wages in the manufacture of clothing are generally lower than in other manufacturing sectors. Statistics Canada reports that in 1977, the average hourly wage for garment workers was $4.23, compared to an average wage of $6.38 in all Canadian manufacturing.

❧

Doris Sklar sits at her desk in the small, crowded office of the clothing firm she has operated for the past ten years. The walls are covered with her advertisements in trade papers and with press clippings illustrating fashion designs she has manufactured. She boasts of the recognition her designs have received, proudly citing export orders from retail stores across Canada and around the world.

These days, Doris Sklar's business is based entirely upon the labour of homeworkers. Doris Sklar's "factory" consists of her office, a cutting room, a shipping section and a work area with two industrial sewing machines. The cutter, an immigrant from Hong Kong, is the only employee on the premises. A few days each week, she is joined by another employee, an experienced sewing machine operator. The operator assembles sample designs, which home sewers then use as models for stitching up dresses from bundles of pre-cut garments. When the operator makes up the samples, Doris Sklar times how long it takes her to do each one and calculates a piece rate, which is then paid to homeworkers for each completed garment. She bases these calculations on a minimum wage rate of $3.30 an hour; if the experienced operator can complete two dresses in an hour, then the piece rate for all homeworkers making that style is set at $1.65 a dress.

Doris Sklar operates a relatively small-scale business, employing between 15 and 20 homeworkers. She says that using homeworkers is the only way she can make money in such a competitive business — the only way to compete with imports produced with cheap, Third World labour. She claims that if she paid her workers more, she would be unable to stay in business.

When she first started, Doris Sklar had a conventional factory loft, with facilities and space for many sewing machine operators.

It was hard enough finding women who could sew a straight seam. Then, after I would spend weeks, sometimes months, training them to do the work, they would quit on me. After some years, I began to use more homeworkers. My first homeworkers were my own inside workers who were housebound after having babies. Gradually, I began to rely more on homeworkers, less on the inside workers. When my factory rent was raised, I decided to get rid of the inside workers altogether, and to just use homeworkers, and I moved into these smaller, cheaper premises.

Nowadays, Doris Sklar recruits her homeworkers through want ads in the local Chinese-language newspaper. Her Chinese-speaking cutter answers the telephone replies, interviews applicants in Chinese and instructs them in procedures. From then on, all the work is done at home.

⚬

The poor working conditions of workers inside Canada's clothing factories have received considerable attention. Every so often, a journalist takes a job in one of the garment factories and writes of the deplorable conditions and the pressure of piecework.[4] Yet relatively little information has come out about the conditions faced by homeworkers in Canada and any recommendations that have been made on this issue have been largely ignored.

In 1970, the Report of the Royal Commission on the Status of Women noted that there were serious problems with the conditions of homework performed by thousands of women in Canada. The report recommended conducting an investigation of homework. To date, no such investigation has been carried out. Homework is still a secret phenomenon, hidden in the basements and closets of the nation.

In 1979, Ontario's Joint Task Force on Immigrant Women issued a report acknowledging that homework "is being exploited by some manufacturers who do not meet minimum wage requirements, fail to recognize hours worked and do not provide some of the additional benefits required by law for the work-force." That task force recommended "a more strict enforcement of the *Employment Standards Act,* including such provisions as the minimum wage standard and vacation pay benefits," and that the Ministry of Labour "give intensive study to the plight of homeworkers to protect them from exploitation."[5] There has been no action taken on these recommendations, and the situation of homeworkers remains the same.

Canada is not the only industrialized country in which there is an underclass of female homeworkers. In the United States, the International Ladies' Garment Workers' Union, which has had a long history of battling homework, has launched a campaign against the growing number of illegal sweatshops in New York, New Jersey and California. These unlicensed factories also tend to employ large numbers of homeworkers. The ILGWU is attempting to shut down all of these illegal factories. Similar campaigns have been launched in England and Australia, where groups have been organizing to extend and enforce employment standards so that homeworkers will not continue to be underpaid and overworked.

Such campaigns are only partly altruistic. Certainly the abhorrent working conditions of homeworkers anger many advocates of fair and decent labour practices. An additional motivating factor, however, is that all clothing workers are threatened by the existence of workers who work under substantially poorer conditions than the rest of the labour force. In part, homeworkers serve to keep down the wages of other clothing workers.

But the decline in the Canadian garment industry that has been continuing steadily since 1977 — largely the result of the extensive increases in imported clothing — means that the unions are not operating from a position of strength. A 1977 report of the Textile and Clothing Board showed that between 1972 and 1977 the number of Canadian clothing establishments dropped from 1,895 to 1,660. This downturn meant a loss of 6,971 jobs, a seven per cent decrease in employment for the industry.[6] So although it seems that it would be in the unions' best interests to ban homework entirely, their energies are concentrated elsewhere, on keeping their own jobs. In the absence of strong union initiatives, reformers must look to government control and regulation to limit the exploitation of homeworkers.

What are the conditions that create and sustain the homework system of production? What are the further conditions that determine the degree to which standards can be imposed on the employment conditions of homework? What should be done to ensure that homeworkers do not work under substandard conditions for subminimum wages? This book attempts to provide answers to these questions, beginning with a look at the historical background of the homework system.

2 THE ORIGINS OF
INDUSTRIAL HOMEWORK

COMMISSIONER:

Are there many shops or places where clothing is made that do not come under the provisions of the Factory Act?

WITNESS:

Hundreds of them.

WITNESS: *What the Commissioner should do to satisfy himself is to walk up and down Bay Street for a few hours any day and see the great number of women staggering up and down with great bundles of clothing; some of the poor creatures hardly able to walk. . .*

INSPECTOR: *I remember one shop where we went and the wages paid ranged from $1 to $3.50 per week for a finisher. When asking the employer how they could sustain themselves on such small means he replied that he only got thirty-seven and a half cents each for making coats and could not afford to give any higher wages.*

(Report on the Sweating System in Canada, 1895)[1]

More than 80 years later, homeworkers can still be seen on Toronto's streets, barely a mile from the places described in the 1895 report. Today they may pick up their piecework by taxi or deliver the finished goods in a neighbour's or relative's car, but their position in relation to other Canadian workers has hardly improved. They are still at the bottom of the economic ladder, toiling long hours at or below the minimum wage. They enjoy fewer social benefits (unemployment insurance, health insurance) than other workers, and have less protection against abuses by employers.

How is it possible that the technological and social changes of the past eight decades have had so little effect on homeworkers? Why have their conditions of employment changed so little compared to those of other workers? To answer these questions, one must understand the origins of homework, and the historic conditions that have defined it.

When we think of the Industrial Revolution, the first picture that comes to mind is of a large, mechanized factory with hundreds or even thousands of employees. The factory may be seen in a positive or negative light, as a symbol of progress or a "dark satanic mill," but for most readers modern industry means large-scale enterprises, assembly lines, heavy machinery and a minute division of labour.

The words "cottage industry," on the other hand, conjure up quite a different image: hand labour, small-scale production and craftsmanship. Many of us suppose that these are the characteristics of a bygone era, before the development of the factory. We picture the independent handcraft worker as overwhelmed by the cheaper, more efficient methods of factory production, forced to give up his or her trade and abandon the comforts of the cottage for a place in an assembly line.

There is more than one grain of truth in this widely-held stereotype, yet it masks some of the most important characteristics of the Industrial Revolution. Although it is true that factories revolutionized production in many industries, their influence was not uniform or consistent throughout the years of the Industrial Revolution, or from one industry to another. In certain fields of industry, producers lost their independence long before mechanized factories were ever built. In others, the growth of mechanized production actually created a demand for new types of cottage industry. In still other cases, home-based production continued to flourish side by side with factories, and came to play an important part in their operations.

To understand the homework industries of today, one must first recognize the role of cottage industry and homework in the earliest years of the Industrial Revolution. In England and most European countries, the story began in the Middle Ages, when craft guilds were formed to protect and regulate the producers of various goods. Through the system of apprenticeship, the guilds carefully controlled admission to each particular craft or trade. In each guild the master craftsmen formed a closed corporation that fixed the quality and quantity of goods to be produced, and assigned each member specific prices and quotas which could not be exceeded.

Although this system worked fairly well in times of scarcity and low consumption, many people found it too restrictive. Women in particular were shut out of the guild trades almost completely. As wives and daughters of master craftsmen, they sometimes took an active part in production, but even if they equalled the men in skill they could only work under their fathers' (or husbands') control. If a craftsman died, his widow was not allowed to continue the business except by marrying another guild member.

Apprentices and journeymen craftsmen also resented the system, because it forced them to wait years or even decades before they could become masters in their own right. Consumers objected to the high prices set by the guilds, and merchants sought to bypass or compete with the guilds by offering non-guild products at lower prices. As a result of all these pressures, new centres of production began to arise in opposition to the guilds. Because the guilds were most strongly entrenched in the cities, their competitors turned their attention to the countryside, where many small agricultural producers were willing to take on part-time work at lower wages than the guilds would allow.

This system of cottage production was especially well suited to the textile industry. As early as the fifteenth and sixteenth centuries, enterprising middlemen were operating in rural areas of England in competition with the clothiers' guilds of the larger cities. From the outset these "putters out" relied on an elaborate division of labour. Cottagers in one village would specialize in spinning wool or flax into yarn, which would then be taken to another village to be woven into cloth. Bleaching, dyeing and finishing of the woven cloth were likewise specialties of particular regions of the countryside. At each stage of production the putter-out provided the raw or semifinished material to workers, and paid them a piecework rate for each unit of yarn or cloth they processed. A successful middleman might deal with hundreds of workers scattered over an area of many square miles.

Many of the cottage producers were women or children, who worked at home while their husbands and fathers farmed. The word "spinster" originally referred to the operators of spinning wheels — often unmarried women who lived with their parents or siblings and took on outside work as their contribution to the household budget. Cottage industry offered such people wages and a degree of independence not available from farming.

The putting-out system enabled many rural families to supplement their meagre agricultural earnings, and in this sense it was a positive development. At the same time, however, it made workers dependent on an entrepreneur for their livelihood. Knowing only one part of the productive process, they were in a weak position negotiating wages. Individual producers were isolated from one another and from the consumers to whom the finished cloth was eventually sold. Their work, moreover, often required little skill or experience, and the employer could always threaten to take his business elsewhere if workers objected to his terms. The worker, on the other hand, was strongly attached to his or her native village, which offered at least a small measure of security in subsistence agriculture. To travel elsewhere in search of higher wages was a risk that few workers were willing to take.

Thus, in various branches of production, cottage industry had many of the features of a factory system. The individual producer was not an independent artisan, but rather a semiskilled wage labourer — a cog in a larger machine, over which he or she had little control. The invention of new machinery, far from challenging this system, actually reinforced it. Some of the earliest breakthroughs in technology, such as the knitting frame and the spinning jenny, were designed for use in a decentralized cottage industry. Only in the later stages of the Industrial Revolution did employers adopt the heavy equipment and centralized production system of the modern factory.

The pace of change was very uneven, varying from one industry to another, and from region to region. Often labour-saving inventions were ignored for many years because employers considered old methods of production more profitable. When labour was abundant and cheap, there was little incentive to invest in expensive machinery. Moreover, if producers worked in their own homes, employers could avoid the expense of building or maintaining factories.

On the other hand, if traditional methods proved awkward or unprofitable, entrepreneurs were more likely to look for alternatives. This is exactly what happened in the cotton industry in the eighteenth century. The consumer demand for cloth was growing so rapidly that traditional producers could barely keep up with it. The difficulty was especially great in the spinning industry. The traditional hand-operated spinning wheel worked so slowly that it took seven full-time spinners to keep one weaver supplied with yarn. Employers found themselves forced to distribute their goods over an ever wider area of the countryside, and coordinating the work of spinners, weavers, bleachers and dyers became almost impossible. In this situation, the invention of mechanized spinning machines seemed a godsend, for they enabled a single worker to spin dozens, then hundreds of strands of yarn at once. One worker could produce as much thread or yarn in a day as a cottage spinner could manufacture in weeks or even months. The advantages of the power mill proved irresistible to employers, and by the early 1800s the cottage spinning industry had moved from cottage to factory.

One might expect that once the new machines were in place in the spinning industry the other branches of cotton production would immediately switch over into mechanized production. In fact this change did not occur for more than a generation. Instead of ending the putting-out system, the improved spinning machines actually brought about a temporary expansion of homework. The employers now possessed an almost limitless supply of yarn, but it still had to be woven into cloth. Inventors had begun experimenting with mechanized looms in the early eighteenth century, but by 1825 the power loom had not yet been perfected. Workers, moreover, still viewed the factories with suspicion, and were much more willing to take on work that they could do in their own homes. For all these reasons, many entrepreneurs chose to expand their traditional networks in the countryside, and the number of home weavers in England soared to more than 250,000. This number included many ex-spinners, who switched to weaving when their former trade moved to the mechanized mills.

Thus the cotton-spinning factories, instead of suppressing homework, created a vast new demand for home weaving. This was true not just in England, but in several other European countries, such as Russia, where cotton weaving was previously unknown. Exports of British yarn created new opportunities for entrepreneurs, and soon tens of thousands of European peasants were weaving at home for piecework wages.

The boom in weaving, however, was shortlived. By the early 1840s, power looms were improved to the point where home production could no longer compete. Some workers tried to resist by smashing the new machines; others accepted lower and lower wages until they could no longer support themselves. Employers took advantage of this situation by offering homeworkers part-time work at seasons of peak demand, thereby expanding production without the expense of additional machinery. Even so, the number of home weavers plummeted, until by mid-century fewer than 10,000 of the original 250,000 remained in the trade.

In other branches of textile production — wool, linen and silk — mechanization was a slower process and homework continued to the end of the nineteenth century. This was partly for technical reasons — other fibres being less suitable to machine processing — but mainly because these industries were experiencing less growth than cotton. Cotton fabrics were on the whole cheaper, more comfortable and more colourful than other textiles, and the cotton industry grew rapidly at the expense of its competitors. Without an expanding market, producers of other fabrics had less reason to introduce new machinery. Instead they tried to compete by driving down the wages of homeworkers. Women and children were hired instead of men, and semiskilled labour was substituted for the work of experienced artisans. Although producers continued to work at home, the conditions of their labour became more and more unhealthy and exploitative:

> Perhaps a more wretched class of workmen never existed than the old woolcombers. The work was all done in their own houses, the best part of their cottages being taken up with it. The whole family . . . worked together round a "combpot" heated by charcoal, the fumes of which had a very deleterious effect upon their health. When we add that the workshop was also perforce the

bedroom, it will not be wondered that woolcombers were almost invariably haggard looking . . . many of them not living half their days.

(Cleckheaton, England, circa 1835)[2]

In the textile industry, then, the creation, destruction or survival of homework depended mainly on the actions of entrepreneurs and employers. From the beginning the industry was organized on a large scale for distant markets. The cottage workers, far from being independent artisans, were mainly wage workers, subordinate to employers and often subjected to severe exploitation. They were part of a factory system, labouring under even worse conditions than their fellow workers in the mills.

The same could be said of many other branches of industry that relied on homework: boot-making, cigar-rolling, nail- and chain-making, lace-making. The most conspicuous example of homework in the late nineteenth century, however, was the garment industry — itself a product of the revolutionary changes in textile manufacturing.

In earlier times most tailors and seamstresses produced made-to-measure garments for wealthy customers. Poor people owned few garments — for many, the old phrase, "only the clothes on his back" was not far from the truth — and those that they had were likely woven and sewn by members of their own families. The Industrial Revolution, however, made available an abundance of cheaper machine-made fabrics. At the same time cities were growing, markets were expanding and the lifestyles of middle-class and working people were changing dramatically. A new clothing industry came into being, producing cheap, standardized garments for mass consumption. It quickly spread, moreover, from the older industrial nations to the New World, where fast-growing cities such as New York, Montreal and Toronto soon became important centres of the garment trade.

Unlike the older system of custom tailoring, the new garment industry relied on a mass of unskilled or semi-skilled workers. Instead of producing a whole garment from start to finish, each worker was given a single task to perform over and over, and the goods would be passed from one worker to another in a kind of assembly line.

Clothes were manufactured on consignment for retail shops, department stores or wholesalers, few of which had any direct contact with workers. Instead they gave out contracts to "jobbers" or subcontractors who would distribute pre-cut materials to small workshops or home-workers at piecework rates. Contracts were awarded to the lowest bidder, and this had the effect of forcing wages almost below subsistence levels. This was the notorious

"sweating system":
> An ordinary small frame building, with two large rooms on the ground floor. The front one was filled with five girls, one a mere child, and four young men [making vests]: the family . . . were washing themselves, and eating breakfast in the room behind, there being a wide open space between the two rooms. . . . He had contracted to make the vests complete at from 17 to 25 cents each: the cloth was supplied him, but he had to provide his own thread and silk, and have the garments sent for and delivered. . . . He worked frequently till midnight, and was always up at sunrise. He did not say what he paid his hands, who worked ten hours a day, but admitted that after paying them he was scarcely able to clear enough to keep his family clothed and fed. They looked, indeed, as though both had been wanting for some time.
>
> (Toronto, 1897)[3]

The term "sweated labour" did not necessarily mean homework. It referred to any situation in which piecework wages were so low that workers had to keep going at a gruelling pace for many hours at a time. Sometimes this work was performed in a workshop under the direct supervision of a subcontractor. Just as often, however, the workers took pre-cut fabrics home so that other members of their families could join in the work.

> The work often has to be fetched every day, or rather the women have to go every day to see if there is anything for them, obviously with no guarantee that their journey will not be in vain. One of the women said that she was often kept waiting several hours before the work was given out, as the master went round each day to collect orders, which he might or might not find quickly.
>
> (Manchester, 1915)[4]

When the work was finished they would return it to the jobber, who would pay them a fixed rate for every dozen garments they delivered. In Canada at the end of the nineteenth century, wages of less than five dollars per week were usual, and few if any homeworkers in the garment industry were earning more than ten dollars. They had to pay for their own machines and thread, and were responsible for transporting the materials to and from the suppliers. Their wages, moreover, were liable to be reduced through fines if the employer found fault with their work.

> When an employee in a factory or contractor's shop does imperfect work, necessitating an alteration, only the time required to make the alteration is lost. On the other hand, a person working at home must carry the goods back again, frequently losing half a day because of having to make an alteration which in actual work only requires a few minutes of time. To avoid this they are often willing to submit to a fine or reduction of wages far in excess of what the making of the alteration would be worth to them.
>
> (Toronto, 1895)[5]

This system was different from the older forms of homework in one crucial respect: it was carried on in cities instead of rural villages. Any advantages a cottage weaver or spinner might have enjoyed — fresh air, a garden or the opportunity for part-time work in agriculture — were lacking in the new setting. Homeworkers were crowded into slums and tenements. Whole families lived and worked in a single room, with poor ventilation and dismal sanitary conditions. Lighting was minimal, heating often inadequate, and plumbing primitive or nonexistent.

> A woman with a large family, some of whom were sick, was the next person we visited . . . the clothes at which she had been working were lying with a heap of rubbish on the dirty floor. She could hardly speak with a consumptive cough, which is fast taking her life away. . . . A little girl, sixteen years of age, who was thin and sickly in appearance, stood by her side and related how she had

worked for eight years past . . . most of the time at two dollars per week. She now intended to help her mother at the machine.

(Toronto, 1897)[6]

Why would anyone put up with such conditions? In the first place, most homeworkers were unskilled workers whose choice of jobs was limited by their background. Some were recent immigrants, unfamiliar with the laws, the opportunities or even the language of their adopted country. Such people often preferred to make contact with the labour market through a fellow countryman even though he might be offering a lower wage.

An educated Italian girl who had been in the United States only five years had been particularly embarrassed by her ignorance of English. Recently she had returned to the only factory in which she had been employed before her marriage, this time to get home work. She was distressed to find that during her short absence the "nice Italian boss" under whom she had worked had left, and she had trouble in understanding the directions of the new one about embroidery.

(Philadelphia, 1930)[7]

In the second place, many homeworkers were mothers of young children. By staying at home they could give their children at least a certain measure of care and supervision, and devote some part of their day to household tasks. Their children, moreover, could be brought into the work at a tender age of four or five:

Her husband used to be in the [steel] mill, but one of his hands was crippled and he lost his job. . . . The rent on the crazy little shack was only $3.50, but food was a serious item. The result was that husband and wife began to make jeans at home, and as fast as the children could hold a needle they were pressed into service. Besides the two oldest children, the second boy and a girl of thirteen now work at the machines, and the others who are still younger sew on buttons, make buttonholes, and pull out threads. The hours of work seem incredible, from four in the morning until nine at night, one steady drive for every member of the household. The output is only fifteen to twenty dozen pairs of jeans a week at best, which brings an income for the family of $16 to $22.

(Pittsburgh, 1915)[8]

If the parents had worked outside the home, enlisting their children to help them with their work would have been more difficult (and, by the early twentieth century, impossible). Another main group of homeworkers consisted of elderly or partially disabled persons who took up piecework because they were unable to cope with the rigours of factory routines.

In many cases the homeworkers were wives or children of wage earners, and this also helps to account for the outrageously low wages they accepted. If they saw themselves as supplementing the earnings of a family breadwinner, then any rates, no matter how meagre, were attractive. Family ties made homeworkers vulnerable in another way as well: so long as the head of the family was gainfully employed, his relatives could not travel very far in search of work, but were likely to content themselves with whatever employment they could find close to home.

Like their counterparts in the weaving industry a century earlier, the homeworkers of the garment industry were closely tied to factory production. Many employers relied on a combination of inside (that is, factory) and outside labour, using the latter as a "reserve army" that could be called upon in seasons of peak demand. Homework enabled the factory owners to adjust production to rising and falling consumer demand without maintaining idle facilities. Factory buildings and equipment could be kept going through the year, while homeworkers were hired or laid off — at no cost to the owners — to meet the changing needs of the seasons.

> To recruit help, agents from the factories sometimes made the rounds of the immediate neighbourhood. "A girl from the factory came ringing the doorbell." "She walks to the houses and asks the ladies if they want to do it [home sewing]." She says, "The work so easy to do; children like it; so easy to get; stay home and work and make the money."
>
> (Philadelphia, 1930)[9]

> Seven of the Fifth Avenue shops send out all their work, and for five factories a part of the work is done outside. The total of these home workrooms, when times are prosperous, ranges up to three thousand dozen pairs of jeans in one week.
>
> (Pittsburgh, 1915)[10]

The combination of inside and outside work had another advantage for employers, in that it gave them an excuse for keeping everyone's wages low. If the inside workers demanded better terms or threatened to go on strike, their bosses would give the work to outworkers, who were bound to be more submissive. The same arguments could be used to play one homeworker off against another: "You don't like it, don't take it." Separate from one another, with no reliable means of gathering information or collectively presenting grievances, homeworkers were rarely able to resist the employers' tactics.

The result was that homeworkers' earnings were much lower than inside workers' wages. In Toronto in the 1890s, female homeworkers were paid as little as $.75 or $1 per week, at a time when male tailors in larger shops were earning as much as $12 per week. The homeworkers were also more likely to be laid off without warning, and to be cheated by their employers.

I learned of one contractor . . . who makes a practice of employing "learners" who engage to work for him without wages while they are learning the trade. These learners, usually girls, are kept at some trivial and easily mastered work . . . and then, when the term for which they agreed to work without wages expires, they are discharged . . . their places being filled by other "learners" who are in turn defrauded out of several months of work and time.

(Toronto, 1895)[11]

If a dispute ever arose between the employer and the worker, the homeworker had no choice but to accept her boss's terms. In Philadelphia in the 1920s, the lowest-paid workers were those who sorted and packaged pins and sewing supplies:

They were two days getting their first allotment done, and were making so little that everyone hurried. The mother scolded, she whipped the children to make them

work, and when the [materials] were brought to the factory they were under weight . . . but as no more could be found they had to forfeit 10 of the 27 cents that they had expected for their two days' work.

(Philadelphia, 1930)[12]

Toward the beginning of the twentieth century, the situation in homework in North America was assailed from several directions: by trade unions, journalists, social reformers, politicians and even by some factory owners. The unions, composed mainly of inside workers, recognized that better wages and hours could be achieved by restricting the use of outwork and sweated labour. "Muckrakers" such as Jacob Riis and Lewis Hine in the United

States did much to publicize the squalor and misery of homeworkers' lives. Public inquiries and parliamentary investigations were held, and bills were introduced to restrict and regulate the abuses of the homework system.

The attack on sweated labour took several different forms. In some localities, attempts were made to outlaw the use of hired labour in private homes. This tactic was effective against one type of sweatshop, in which the jobber or subcontractor crowded a dozen or so workers into a single room. Once these places were defined as factories under the law, they were required to meet the same standards of safety and health as larger establishments: proper heating and ventilation, control of hazardous materials and dangerous equipment, provision of toilet facilities and running water. Many smaller establishments could not afford to do this, and were forced to close their doors. In most cases, however, homeworkers who employed no one but members of their own families were exempted from the provisions of the law. Their work — the most poorly paid, most exploitative of all — was not affected by the new provisions.

> The large number of homework families, the temporary nature of their work, the constant shifting of residence of families at the poverty level, the difficulty of obtaining true addresses for families on relief rolls, the carelessness and ignorance of some employers, and the economic advantage to them from concealment of the facts, all operate against effective regulation. . .
>
> (New York, circa 1935)[13]

Similar difficulties arose whenever reformers tried to extend other provisions of the factory laws to homeworkers. The laws themselves were often half-hearted and ineffectual — for example, Manitoba's 1913 *Factories Act,* which only required factory inspectors to "as far as possible see that such [home] work is performed under sanitary conditions." Even when stronger laws were passed, enforcement was almost impossible. It was hard enough to restrict the hours of work at proper factories, or to forbid the employment of young children at hazardous jobs. Once the work was carried on at home, the problems increased a hundredfold. Factory inspectors (as well as social workers and public health inspectors) were appointed to make sure that the laws were followed, but they were few in number, unable to visit every street or every home where women and children might be working illegally. Unscrupulous employers could always falsify their records to make it seem that they had followed the letter of the law, and homeworkers who valued their jobs were not about to expose them. Worst of all were the "fly by night" firms that shifted their operations from place to place to escape detection. A Toronto factory inspector's report in 1895 was characteristic:

> Last summer walking up a street in "the wards" I heard machines going in a house. I went in and found a place I had not previously known of. I inspected it. I went again two weeks after and found that the man had skipped and left his employees without paying them their wages.
> (Toronto, 1895)[14]

Another tactic that helped to restrict the use of homework was the system of labelling "tenement goods." Critics of sweated labour blamed the system for spreading contagious diseases from the workers' homes to the consumers who bought the finished products. Several American states, including New York, Massachusetts and Illinois, passed laws in the 1890s requiring that such goods be identified with a special label, so that the public would be warned of the hazard. Understandably, few consumers were willing to put their health at risk, and sales of labelled merchandise plummeted. (This campaign, incidentally, was supported by some factory-owners, who resented the competition from sweatshops.) If the law had been uniformly enforced, it would probably have abolished homework altogether. Employers of sweated labour, however, were quick to find ways of avoiding the requirements. Some moved their operations to other states where laws were less stringent, while others concocted various systems of shipping the garments from state to state in order to conceal their true origin.

Labelling homework goods as hazardous was unsuccessful as a method for controlling sweated labour. In later years, however, as the trade union movement gained strength in the garment industry, the reverse of the original strategy was attempted. Instead of singling out the products of sweated labour as dangerous to health, a union label was used as a seal of approval for clothes that had been sewn under union contract. This method of labelling was easier to enforce, but its success in affecting consumers' buying patterns was hard to demonstrate, and many non-union firms continued to flourish.

Although none of these systems was entirely successful as a method of outlawing the abuses of homework, the total number of homeworkers declined from the 1890s onwards. Certainly the efforts of labour unions and social reformers played an important role in the decline, but it would be a mistake to see them as the sole source of change. Rather, the homework system was abandoned by employers when it ceased to fulfill their needs. For many this point was reached when the efficiencies of factory labour outweighed the cheapness of home labour. The immediate cause might be the introduction of new machinery, the efficiency of assembly-line production or even the inconveniences of giving out homework. As unions and governmental regulations became more effective, various aspects of homework were increasingly restricted in ways

that, though they could not prevent its use, made it less attractive to employers.

The incentive to hire homeworkers would have been much greater, however, had the lives of the workers themselves not been changing over these same years. Workers, especially married women, had originally taken up homework because of a desperate need for money.

The inquiry as to why she worked seemed superfluous. With a gesture indicating the children and the furnishings of the small, crowded room she replied: "Why I work? Needed a slice of bread . . ." Her husband was a street cleaner, earning at the most $25 a week and in winter sometimes only $10. He had had four serious illnesses and by her homework earnings the wife probably kept the roof over their heads.

(Philadelphia, 1930)[15]

Whenever that need diminished, whenever the proportion of weak and vulnerable members of society declined for any reason, the supply of willing hands also went down. The drop in homework was directly related to long-term trends in the economy and social policy. Improvements in social services and minimum wage laws enabled many homeworkers to shift into better-paying jobs outside the home. Those who were housebound or dependent, on the other hand, benefitted from other changes in the economy and society. In times of full employment and rising wages, other members of their households were able to bring home bigger paychecks, making the homeworkers' earnings less necessary for their families' needs. In other cases, improved welfare and public assistance programs provided enough security that people could afford to refuse the most exploitative forms of homework. If homework was a response to poverty, then any reduction in the levels of poverty was likely to reduce the number of homeworkers.

By the same token, any social or economic change that increased the number of impoverished families was likely to drive more workers back to homework. It is no accident that homework industries have never been wholly eliminated, or that they have followed an up-and-down course in recent decades.

Homework seems to have declined between 1900 and 1920, due in part to the garment unions' success in organizing inside workers, and in part to the economic and social effects of the First World War: full employment, higher wages and a shortage of male factory labour, due to the large numbers of men in military service. During the war many women took jobs outside the home, but after the war most returned to the role of housewife, and the system of industrial homework began to revive. For some North Americans the 1920s were a time of prosperity, but many others experienced unemployment and a falling standard of living. Labour unions encountered stiff resistance and conservative governments in Canada and the United States were unwilling to interfere in the relations between workers and employers. Under these conditions homework again began to flourish, and as the world economy sagged in the late 1920s the trend became even stronger.

With the onset of the Great Depression in 1929, millions of people found themselves out of work and willing to accept any job, no matter how temporary or poorly paid. For manufacturers, facing a shrinking market for their goods, homework became a means of cutting costs. Once again homework was associated with widespread poverty and suffering. Eventually, however, the public outcry against these conditions became too loud to be ignored. Governments in Canada, the United States and Great Britain were obliged to take new steps to deal with the economic crisis. These included social insurance, job creation programs and fair labour standards laws to regulate wages, hours and terms of employment. Among these reforms were new restrictions on the use of industrial homework.

In the 1930s, governments took their first hesitant steps toward effective regulation. One of the first to act was the province of Ontario, where laws of 1936 and 1937 required homeworkers and employers to obtain permits for their trade. The permits were issued by factory inspectors, who could inspect payroll records and workshops, and could cancel a permit if they thought a worker was not being paid the province's minimum wage. Even so, homeworkers were not given the same protection as other workers in Ontario. Factory workers' wages were supervised by a special division of the Ministry of Labour, but the homeworkers' only protection came from a small number of inspectors who were burdened with many other duties. (More than 30 years later, in 1968, the *Minimum Wage Act* of Ontario was finally rewritten to include homeworkers.)

Similar laws were passed in British Columbia and in eighteen American states in the 1930s. National regulation was also attempted in the U.S. under the *National Recovery Act* of 1933, which set up labour-management committees to govern employment in each major industry. Quebec's *Minimum Wage Act* of 1941 applied to "every employee working in the Province, whether at his employer's, at home, or elsewhere." In spite of all these steps, however, homework continued to be abused. An investigation in Pennsylvania in 1934-35, for example, found that almost 80 per cent of all the permits issued to homeworkers had been violated as to hours, wages and child labour. The provisions of homework laws were almost impossible to enforce, as a study of homework in Rhode Island illustrated:

> The regulation of hours of work that has been successfully enforced for factory workers . . . is obviously out of the question as far as homeworkers are concerned. Paid by the piece, homeworkers are tempted to put in longer hours of work than would be permitted in the factory, and they often work far into the night. . . . The prevention of child labour also is practically impossible under a system of industrial homework. It is a temptation in families that eke out their existence by homework to increase their pitifully small earnings with the aid of even very small children. . . [16]

Inspectors could issue permits and inspect payroll records, but they could not go into every home to supervise every homeworker's labour. Neither could they rely on the workers themselves to complain when the law was being broken. A worker who valued her job was sure to keep her mouth shut.

Could adequate standards for homework ever be enforced? According to the Industrial Commissioner of New York State in 1941:

> The overwhelming majority of American government officials who have ever had anything to do with the administration of [homework laws] . . . are firmly convinced that it can never be satisfactorily regulated. Low wages, long hours, child labour, unhealthy and unsanitary working conditions . . . are part and parcel of the system . . . complete abolition alone can eliminate them.[17]

This view was shared by a majority of witnesses who testified at the U.S. Labor Department's hearings on homework in 1941. Labour unions, state and federal officials, and even manufacturers argued that the time had come to put an end to all homework. In response, the department drew up a new set of rules, outlawing homework in women's apparel and six other industries that had been the biggest users of home labour. True, the rules only applied to larger firms that engaged in interstate commerce, but they marked a turning point in the history of homework in the United States — the beginning of a downward trend that would last for more than 30 years.

The decline in homework that followed was caused not just by the Labor Department's action, but also by economic trends. With the end of the Depression, poverty and unemployment were greatly reduced, and fewer women needed to work at home to support their families. During the Second World War, thousands of women took up jobs outside the home, in factories and government agencies that paid far better wages than homework. The 1940s and 1950s brought widespread prosperity, suburbanization and a new style of life. More women stayed at home with their families, but fewer of them needed to look for wages as homeworkers. A report from North Carolina in the mid-fifties showed a clear connection between a rising standard of living and a drop in homework: as the minimum wage for other forms of employment went up, the number of homeworkers in the state went down steadily.

Even so, the practice of homework was never completely eliminated. It continued to flourish in low-income communities, and to attract as workers the most vulnerable and dependent individuals — for example, recent immigrants, disabled persons, mothers of young children. In some large cities in Canada and the United States, unregistered aliens (illegal immigrants) became a major source of home labour. Unable to work openly, they were easy prey for homework contractors, who kept no payroll records and paid them only a fraction of the legal minimum wage. Welfare recipients were another group that could be exploited in this way. One woman in New York's South Bronx reported in 1980 that her employer deducted six per cent from her pay every week, not for taxes or social security but "for giving me the privilege of working off the books."

Thus, although homework declined for several decades, the need for surveillance remained. A top U.S. official admitted in the late 1950s that if enforcement efforts were relaxed for even a year or two, the problem of homework would re-emerge. Fifteen years later, this is exactly what has happened in the United States. By most accounts, the number of sweatshops and illegal homeworkers in the United States has soared since 1970, with an estimated total of 50,000 to 70,000 persons working under illegal conditions in New York alone, another 100,000 in the U.S. mid-west and an indeterminate number on the west coast.[18] In a time of recession and uncertainty, when more and more people have been attracted to homework, state and federal agencies have sharply reduced the number of field inspectors. In New York State in 1976, the number of factory inspectors was cut by 45 per cent, leaving a total of 15 people to deal with all fair labour standards violations in the state.

Ironically, this trend has come at a time when many politicians are trying to cut back the government's involvement in labour standards. As a presidential candidate, Ronald Reagan made "de-regulation" one of his main slogans. Since Reagan's inauguration in January 1980, his Secretary of Labor, Raymond Donovan, has been trying to apply this principle to homework. Donovan admits that large numbers of homeworkers are working illegally and that their conditions of employment are deplorable, but he insists that the 1941 regulations cannot improve the situation. Instead he wants to legalize homework, on the grounds that homeworkers will then be more willing to come forward and denounce employers' abuses. In response to Donovan's proposals, local officials and labour unions have argued that homework will never give workers a decent living. Legalizing homework, they insist, means legalizing one of the worst forms of exploitation.

Some of the strongest opposition to Donovan's proposals has come from the Federation of Apparel Manufacturers, an association of 5,500 factory-based manufacturers. They object that employers of homework would enjoy unfair competitive advantages, paying lower wages and avoiding the other requirements of the fair labour standards laws (overtime, vacation pay, social security). "Homework," argues the Federation's president,

inevitably leads to child labor and to unreported and unpaid hours of employment. . . . The Labor Department's notion that the lifting of the homework ban will actually encourage workers to report wage-hour violations is totally unrealistic. What worker, financially dependent upon a homework employer for her basic subsistence, will be brave enough to report a violation and cut off her only source of income? What unregistered alien will complain to a Federal agency?[19]

As this book goes to press, the Donovan proposals are still being debated in the United States and the outcome is still uncertain. In autumn of 1981, the U.S. Department of Labor took steps to legalize homework in one of the affected industries, knitted outerwear, but this action was immediately challenged in the courts by a coalition of unions and industrial associations. Proposals to allow homework in other industries have been temporarily shelved, but the Reagan administration remains committed to the notion of de-regulation.

In Canada, where homework has been restricted but not outlawed, the total number of homeworkers does not seem to have changed dramatically in the last few years. Some workers obtain legal permits for their work and receive a certain amount of protection under the minimum wage laws. A large number continues to operate outside the law, receiving lower wages and suffering more abuse from employers.

The history of industrial homework suggests several lessons for the 1980s. In the first place, homeworkers have rarely if ever been independent producers. A romanticized picture of cottage industry has no basis in fact. Even the earliest spinners and weavers were exploited, working at the employers' whims, with little control over their own wages or product. Their descendents in the sweatshops and tenements fared no better. Homework has always taken advantage of the downtrodden and defenceless members of society, and homeworkers have remained at the bottom of the economic ladder from the beginning of the Industrial Revolution to the present.

A second lesson is that governmental restrictions have never been entirely effective in controlling or abolishing homework. The nature of the industry is such that, no matter what rules are introduced, someone is bound to find a way of evading them. This points, though, to a third lesson — perhaps the most important of all: homework can only be abolished by abolishing the needs that spawned it. Until all workers can achieve an acceptable standard of living without engaging in ill-paid, unhealthy work, they will continue to be drawn to the homework trades.

3 A CAPTIVE LABOUR FORCE

*T*he contemporary practice of homework in Canada is a story of exploitation. The details of the system are very similar to those of the era before trade unions won working people the rights to minimum wages, overtime pay and

59

benefits such as unemployment insurance. The workers in today's home sweatshops are forced to accept such conditions as fluctuations between 12-hour workdays and slack times with no work and no pay; piecework rates that are not disclosed until after the work has been done; basic rates of pay set far below those paid to workers inside the factories; and penalties for work considered by employers to be substandard. The vulnerable situation of homeworkers enables employers to use antiquated employment practices to maximize their profits at the workers' expense.

The homeworker labour force — like the population of garment workers as a whole — is composed mainly of immigrant women. These workers generally operate at a disadvantage in the labour market, taking the least desirable jobs — those that do not attract Canadian-born workers. In a 1974 manpower analysis of the British Columbia garment industry, B.C.'s Ministry of Labour observed that "the very fact that the industry cannot recruit personnel from the mainstream of the labour force raises some questions regarding working conditions in the industry."[1] More recently, the Canadian Advisory Council on the Status of Women reported on the labour conditions of immigrant women employed in the garment factories of Canadian cities. The report, prepared by Montreal journalist Sheila Arnopoulos, draws a dismal picture of substandard working conditions, low wages and high pressure and stress for the workers.[2]

Poor as the working conditions in the garment industry are for the factory workers, the conditions of employment for homeworkers in the industry are considerably worse. Most homeworkers are able to make the comparison, because most of them have had in-factory experience. They describe a system with two classes of workers — the inside factory workers, who receive regular wages, benefits and overtime pay for overtime hours — and the home-workers, who receive none of these things. Within an industry already known for low wages, high pressure of work and poor working conditions, the homeworkers are extremely disadvantaged.

One homeworker with four years of experience making women's dresses for several different manufacturers provides an account of her conditions of employment:

> The usual rate is $1 to $1.50 for each completed dress. It was higher when I started with this firm last year, but they reduced the rate after a few months. I think they pay us half of what they pay the workers in the factory. And in the factory, they get pay increases.
>
> I work very fast; I'm an experienced seamstress. Recently, I've been making up dresses that are very complicated, and each one takes a long time to complete. I've asked three times for a raise, but I've gotten none. The boss said, "I don't know how long you take. If you take an hour to do half an hour's work, that's your business."
>
> I remember one time last January — I was really shocked. I had done one style of dress — it was fairly complicated, with two seams down the front, two seams down the back, a collar, set-in sleeves and a zipper down the back. I did everything but finish the hem.
>
> Now, I keep track of all the dresses I sew, because I don't know what they will pay me for each style, until I get my cheque at the end of the month. By that time, I might forget what a style was, and how much work it involved. So I keep records, with a sketch of the style and the style number on these little cards.
>
> When I got my cheque for that January, I saw that they had paid me only one dollar for each of those dresses. I phoned to complain, but they just said, "If you had worked more, you would get more." They take advantage of the women who have to work at home. When-

ever I complain, they have only one answer: "If you don't like it, you can leave it."

There is no government control over homework. Is it possible? We get no benefits. I pay the income tax, but I get no benefits. I asked the employer to pay the Canada Pension Plan. He said, "I don't want to be bothered with that, it's your problem." Sometimes, when I am working by myself, I think about the fact that I am getting older and older, and that when I get old, I will have no pension. It is unfair not to give us the same benefits as the women in the factory. In fact, we do better work than they do. We have to do better work, or they just won't bring us any more to do.

This year, there was a big rush period, for the pre-Christmas orders. I had to work evenings and Saturdays. I work overtime, but I don't get paid overtime rates. It is like blackmail, I have to rush, or they won't give me more work.

After they rushed me so much, they realized that there might be errors. Then they covered themselves. I received a letter two weeks ago saying that if they found that I had made any errors, they would deduct an amount for each of the defective articles, because, they said, they would have to pay one of the factory workers to correct the error.

That was what happened to my sister, who also does homework. They said she had done something wrong with the zippers she had sewn in some dresses, and deducted $.30 from each of the dresses she had completed.

It doesn't do any good to change factories. They are all the same. At least this factory has lots of work, more or less regular.

Piecework Rates and Changing Styles

Most homeworkers in the needle trades do not manage to earn even the minimum hourly wage for their work. Rates paid for women's dresses range from $1 up to a high of about $3 a dress, depending on the complexity of the style. Homeworkers receive pre-cut bundles of dresses in styles that often change weekly. With each bundle they receive a finished sample garment to guide their work. They are responsible for the complete assembly of the garments, with the exception of buttons, buttonholes, hems and final pressing, which are done in the factory. The time required to complete a garment can vary from half an hour to two hours, depending on the complexity of the design and the speed of the sewing machine operator. Rates paid for children's wear and for dolls and toys are considerably lower than dress rates. One worker, who has been making children's clothing at home for a year and a half, reports that she is paid $.50 each for shirts and $1.20 for dresses. She estimates her hourly earnings at $2.

Homeworker Cecilia Montana describes how employers set the piece rate.

> They know how to do it. They take a very experienced operator and time her, and base the rate on the minimum wage, so that only an experienced operator can earn even the minimum wage. It makes it very difficult to earn any better than the minimum.
> I am an experienced seamstress. I learned to sew in Italy, and I have been sewing at home for five years. Before that, I worked sewing mattresses in a factory for four years. I am a fast worker. If I was working in a factory now, I would be one of the top earners, at $6 or maybe $6.50 an hour. Now I only make between $3 and $4 an hour.

Changes in clothing fashion affect the fortunes of homeworkers. Because pay rates are set by the piece, it is almost always the case that the amount of money a worker can earn is related directly to the complexity of the garments she sews. The simpler the style, the more she can produce in a day, and the more money she makes. More elaborate, complicated styles do have somewhat higher piece rates. But the differences in rates are not enough to compensate for the longer time they take. For example, one long-time homeworker blamed the "gypsy look" for her meagre earnings of the previous year. "With all those ruffles and long skirts, I only earned $4,500 in the entire year."

The process of sewing a complete garment is slowed down each time a worker has to learn how to construct a new style. While an inside worker in the factory has a supervisor to demonstrate procedures for each new item and to check the first few items completed, the home-worker is generally left to her own resources and to study the sample garment to interpret each new style. In many cases, homeworkers rely on their husbands to pick up the pre-cut bundles of garments from the factory. Sometimes instructions are conveyed through the husbands, who may not be knowledgeable about sewing techniques. Errors are costly — both in time, and in the penalties that are sometimes levied on work that is done imperfectly.

Different employers have different procedures for dealing with errors. Some require a homeworker to come into the factory to "make good" her mistakes. Others deduct a set amount from the piece rate, claiming that they will have to pay another worker to correct the mistakes.

Homeworkers are afraid to refuse a particular job for fear the employer will punish them by withholding work. One worker, a Greek immigrant who has been sewing at home for the same company for the past four years, said that she occasionally refused styles that seemed too complex, or that required machine attachments she did not have. She added, however, that "I can't do that very often, or they won't like me and won't give me work."

In both Ontario and Quebec, labour standards legislation requires employers to pay homeworkers the minimum wage. In neither province is there any guarantee that homeworkers actually earn the minimum wage. Most do not.

❧

Rosa Marchetti works pressing, trimming, folding and packaging uniforms and smocks for a contractor. She is paid $.30 for each garment she completes. Although there is some variation in the styles and complexity of the garments she works on, they are basically similar, and she estimates that she can complete 50 pieces in an eight-hour workday.

At the $.30 piece rate, even if she were given a steady supply of bundles of garments, she could earn only $75 for a 40-hour work week. In fact, there are often shortages of work and a review of Rosa Marchetti's pay stubs over a four-month period in 1980 reveals an average weekly wage of $46.77.

In addition to a low rate of pay, Rosa Marchetti puts up with an unpredictable work flow and considerable pressure from her employer to speed up her production rate.

The boss or his driver will deliver a bundle of 50 smocks one day and will expect to come back the next day to pick them up. I cannot plan my time — I never know when the work will arrive.

He tells me I should work faster, and keeps telling me about some "Mrs. Fernandes" who can press and pack between 100 and 150 garments a day.

Because they work alone, without benefit of contact with other employees, it is virtually impossible for home-workers to judge the degree to which their employers take advantage of them. Rosa Marchetti echoes the sentiments of other isolated homeworkers when she says,

> I don't know any other women doing homework — but I would very much like to. I'd like to know how many gar-ments other women press in a day. I'd like to meet that Mrs. Fernandes — if there really is such a woman!

Added to the problems of low piecework rates and the failure of employers to state specific rates before the work is completed, is a practice whereby employers establish complex and mystifying systems of calculating home-workers' pay. In some cases, the employees do not under-stand the way the employer calculates their earnings. One worker described a method of payment that her employer termed the "bonus system." The basic rate of pay for dresses was between $1.20 and $2.20 per dress. Added to this was a bonus of $.25 for each dress. According to the worker,

> I don't know where this bonus system comes from, or how it works. I don't know if everyone gets the same, or if this is just my rate. They say that in the factory the workers make the same money, but I don't know how to check it.

Louise Lamphere, an anthropologist who worked for half a year as a sewing machine operator in a New England garment factory, offers the following description of a piecework system.

> The piece-rate system used in this plant . . . is based on a complex decimal system that is baffling to the workers since it is not clearly related to the garments bundled in dozens or to minutes that show on wall clocks. The hour is divided into 100 parts and the rates calculated accord-

ingly. For example, 10 minutes is really .167 of an hour, and a piece rate of .073 means that an operation must be performed on a dozen garments in 4.38 minutes if a sewer is to earn the base rate of $3.31 per hour on which the piece rates are figured.[3]

A different, equally complex system of payment is described by a 64-year-old woman working at home as a sock mender. Her job is to fix "irregulars," machine-made garments produced with flaws. She uses a hook to pick up dropped stitches and mend the flaw. After working as a mender in a factory, "sitting on a stool in the mill for eight and a half hours per day for seven years," her health began to suffer, and she decided to work at home.

Here again, the system of reckoning pay is complicated and confusing, but one fact stands out very clearly: to keep her wages from going down she has to work even faster than she did in the factory.

When I left the factory I was getting $3.50 an hour. It was a time rate, but I had to make up my minutes. I had 26 minutes to do a dozen pair of socks. When I started to work at home they cut me down to 23 [that is, she had to do a dozen in 23 minutes to maintain her former pay]. For knee-highs I got 30 minutes. The last batch I did, I got only 22 minutes for doing long socks.

WAGES

During my interviews with them, I asked homeworkers to estimate their wages on an hourly, weekly and annual basis. Despite their irregular work schedules and their employers' attempts at mystification of wage rates, most of the women have calculated their real wage rates. They know that they are underpaid, and that their skills are undervalued. They know too, that the low rates of pay and poor conditions of employment are fairly standard for homework in the garment trades. They realize that they will not be able to improve their earnings significantly until they are able to work outside the home setting.

The majority of homeworkers work full time, at least seven hours a day, five days a week. During the period under study, 1978-80, the average annual rate of pay for a full-time homeworker was $4,136. On a weekly basis, homeworkers' pay averaged just under $100.

The highest wage reported by any of the homeworkers was the $8,000 earned by a samplemaker. Shirley Chung worked for eight years sewing in a factory in Hong Kong before emigrating to Canada; she worked for another ten years inside Toronto's garment factories, and has been doing homework for the past two years. Her relatively high earnings are due mainly to the fact that employers pay more for the sample garments used to collect orders from buyers. The piece rate for the samples ranges from $2 to $5 each. Shirley estimates that in an hour she can complete about two $2.50 items or one $5 one. Her workday is eight and a half hours, from 9 a.m. to noon, 1:30 p.m. to 5 p.m. and from 7 p.m. to 9 p.m. She works seven days a week, when the work is available.

Some comparative statistics on homeworkers' earnings are available from the province of Quebec. The Joint Commission for the Dress Industry there, the body responsible for industrial homework in the women's garment industry, provides annual totals of registered homeworkers, along with the total wages paid to these workers in 1978. A simple average of these figures indicates that on a per capita basis, the Quebec homeworkers were earning an annual salary of $2,797.[4]

Because of the lack of enforcement of labour standards relating to homework, women are sometimes even cheated out of the meagre wages promised them. One homeworker described how she had worked for two months sewing coats for a manufacturer who then went out of business. He paid her with a cheque for $600, which was not honoured. All of her efforts to locate the employer and receive her wages failed.

IRREGULARITY OF WORK

Homeworkers' wages are not only low; they are also irregular and unpredictable. The garment trade is an industry based on a seasonal market. There are several periods during the year when production is slowed down or halted. When homeworkers don't work they don't get paid. Between these slack periods, there are periods of peak demand when the women find themselves working from early morning until late at night, often for six or even seven days a week. May through October are the busiest months. Starting in November, and running through until the end of January, there is little or no work.

Homeworkers in industries aside from the garment trade also suffer from stressful rush orders that alternate with gaps in the work assignments. Doreen Williams, for example, is a homeworker whose irregular workload is attributable to production bottlenecks rather than to seasonal fluctuation in style.

Doreen Williams sews and packages shower caps. Her work involves sewing a circle of elastic thread onto an 18-inch square of thin plastic, and then packing the cap into a plastic envelope. The sewing takes 11 seconds per cap; packaging takes another five seconds. Bundling the caps in batches takes more time.

The employer pays her $15 per 1,000 caps. When there is a rush job — a big order for a hotel, for example — Doreen works seven days a week. There are also slack periods, such as the time her employer ran out of elastic thread that had to be ordered from San Francisco. For two weeks, Doreen had no work and no pay.

&

Homeworkers have virtually no recourse when their flow of materials or supplies slows down or stops. An example of the frustration felt by homeworkers faced with such slowdowns in workflow is provided by Lucy Valente, a homeworker with six years of experience.

Lucy Valente bought herself an industrial sewing machine and began to sew at home six years ago. She sews women's dresses. She is paid about $2 per dress and can turn out two or two and a half dresses per hour, giving her an hourly rate of between $4 and $5. Lucy does not complain about the rate at which she is paid, but wishes that the flow of work and materials would be more regular and more predictable.

Lucy's boss, a small-scale contractor, generally delivers her bundles of 25 dresses on Wednesdays. She is expected to complete these by Monday. This means she works on the weekends but has no work on Mondays and Tuesdays, days when the children are in school. Lucy regrets being unable to use her weekends for family activities.

Even more irritating to Lucy is the casual manner in which the contractor pays her. While she is careful to meet her deadlines, and to have the bundles ready for pick-up at the designated time, her paycheque is frequently delayed, forcing her to phone the employer repeatedly to ask for it. Payment delays of up to six weeks are common.

A more minor but recurring annoyance is the contractor's failure to provide Lucy with enough thread to complete the garments in the bundles. "He doesn't send enough, and then he expects me to supply the thread myself. I tell him that if he keeps it up, I will start sewing the stuff with the wrong colour thread, but that still doesn't do any good."

Expenses

In order to do industrial sewing at home, workers must have their own equipment. A heavy duty industrial sewing machine, which sews much faster than an ordinary home sewing machine, is a requirement of most employers. The cost of these machines ranges from about $300 for a used machine to over $1,000 for a new one. Most of the homeworkers purchase their machines from shops that carry factory equipment and offer service contracts. Workers are completely responsible for the servicing and maintenance of their machines. Servicing fees are at least $50 a year. Machine rental is another option chosen by some of the homeworkers, who cannot afford to purchase a machine. One home sewer reported machine rental costs of $70 for three months.

Without a heavy duty, industrial machine, a homeworker cannot sew fast enough to make much money. One homeworker sews rag dolls on her portable home sewing machine, receiving a dollar for each doll. The employer delivers the front and back section of each doll, printed on fabric. This homeworker's duties include sewing the two parts together, stuffing the doll and sewing a label onto the finished product. Her older children, aged 10 and 12, often help to stuff the dolls. Each doll takes at least 45 minutes to complete. This worker knows that if she had an industrial sewing machine, she would be able to work much faster, and thereby earn a lot more money. However, she comments ironically,

> A factory machine would cost me at least $600. I would have to sew dolls for an entire year just to make enough money to buy the machine.

One Montreal homeworker works primarily on leather coats. She requires two sewing machines; one for sewing leather and another, a regular industrial machine, for making the fabric linings for the coats. The cost of the leather machine was $1,000, and that was for a used, reconditioned model. At the time of the interview, she was still paying it off in installments. The other machine cost her $700. In total, her equipment costs represent a sizeable investment, especially considering that her annual earnings are about $5,000.

One Toronto dress manufacturer uses a particularly devious means of making his workers shoulder machinery costs. If he finds a skilled seamstress who wants to work, but who does not have her own industrial machine, he offers to "advance" her the money, allowing the worker to pay him back in monthly installments by deducting a set amount from each paycheque. In addition to having the workers pay for the machinery, this employer succeeds in compelling the workers to continue working for him — at least until their equipment is paid for.

In addition to the initial capital investment on their equipment, homeworkers must occasionally pay for attachments to do special kinds of seams or trimming, and must regularly supply needles for the machines. As noted earlier, in one case, a worker was expected to purchase her own thread; however, thread is generally provided by the employer. Homeworkers must also pay utility costs which, for the operation of an industrial machine, are considerable.

Michelle LeBlanc, a Montreal homeworker, presses and packs children's garments. As part of the folding operation, she is required to pin the clothes in several places. Her employer, who is supposed to supply all of the necessary equipment, continually gives her too few straight pins, and Michelle is obliged to buy them herself. Whenever she protests, the employer accuses her of wasting the pins he's provided. In the end, of course, she must provide the pins, for until she returns the garments

in finished form, properly packaged, she does not get paid.

The transportation of goods to and from the factory involves additional expenses for most homeworkers. If they drive, there is the cost of gasoline. Many homeworkers do not have access to cars of their own, and are forced to take taxis to deliver heavy bundles of completed garments and to fetch new bundles of work. Workers report spending up to $15 weekly for taxi fares.

The Home as Workplace

An Italian homeworker who has been sewing dresses and jackets at home for the past five years makes the following observation about the home as a workplace:

> People think it's an advantage to work in your own home. They say, "You don't have to go out in the cold." That may be, and it may also be that I save some money on pantyhose and carfare, but I would prefer to go out to work if I could.

These sentiments are shared by most homeworkers. Use of the family home as workspace for industrial sewing creates strains on the household — strains which are felt most by the women themselves.

Most homeworkers live in families in which the responsibility for housekeeping duties rests with women and, to a lesser extent, female children. Industrial sewing is a messy activity, producing a large amount of lint, dust and scraps of fabric, thread, elastic and other trimmings. The women who sew at home find themselves saddled with the usual responsibility for keeping the house in good order, so they must both turn out a high volume of garments and eradicate all traces of sewing activity from their household.

In some cases, family members complain about the disorder created by scraps from the sewing. As one woman explained,

> The static electricity makes the short threads cling to the carpet and get all over the house. My husband and children hate it when the house gets all messy with those threads.

Many of the women report that they vacuum clean their homes several times a day. Although they express some resentment at having to work so hard to clean up the sewing scraps, they share their families' attitudes towards the importance of a clean and tidy home. To these women and their families, the house is an important symbol of family life. One woman put it simply when responding to a compliment on the attractiveness of her home:

> That's why we came to Canada, for a good home like this.

Under these circumstances, the necessity to incorporate industrial machinery and the paraphernalia of clothing production into the home environment is a major source of strain.

Child Labour

In some instances, the practice of homework involves other members of the family. It is invariably a woman who has primary responsibility for homework, but she may be assisted directly by her husband and children. Family involvement takes a number of forms.

Husbands frequently assume responsibility for pickup and delivery of bundles of goods from the factories. These trips can be as far as 15 or 20 miles between home and factory, so such transport often means considerable expenditure of time and money.

Child labour is another form of family participation in homework. It is not uncommon for young children to perform such routine jobs as turning belts, trimming seams and packing up bundles of completed articles. Although child labour legislation has eliminated the full-time employment of school-age children, the practice of homework often results in long hours of part-time work for children.

Location of Workspace

Each of the homeworkers has set up a workspace, generally out of the way of other household activities such as cooking or eating. The most frequent location for homework is a basement. There the women can keep the work set up with a minimum of disruption to the other routines of family life.

An alternative location used by some homeworkers is an enclosed back porch. These areas have the advantage of natural light during daylight hours. Porch work areas have the disadvantage that they are sometimes colder than the rest of the house, as they often have no basement beneath them and poor insulation.

The location of the homeworkers' workplace in dark or unheated basements or porches appears to be symbolic of the level of importance accorded to their work. Within their own families, these women's primary responsibility is ensuring the smooth functioning of the household. Children must receive care and attention; the housework and laundry must be done; meals must be prepared. When their household responsibilities are fulfilled, they can turn their attention to their homework — work that may occupy them for eight, ten or even 12 hours a day or night.

Despite the inhospitable atmosphere of many of the workspaces, many homeworkers decorate them to suit their personal preferences. They use plants, family photographs, children's artwork or religious pictures to ornament their work area. One woman has hung a crucifix on the wall directly above her industrial sewing machine. She says, "When I get tired and depressed, I look up and then I feel better."

HEALTH HAZARDS

In the early years of the homework system in North America, there was a great deal of public concern that the production of garments in the home, under unhygienic conditions, might help spread contagious diseases such as typhoid, scarlet fever, diptheria and smallpox. The media conjured up images of tenement sweatshops in which children sick with communicable diseases were bedded down on bundles of partly-sewn garments. To some extent, this generalized fear inhibited the proliferation of the homework system in North America. In several American states, prior to the turn of the century, legislation was enacted requiring that all garments be labelled to specify the location in which they were made — whether factory, by contractors or in private homes. The tagging system enabled the purchaser to avoid goods that might have been made under unsanitary conditions. It is ironic that the medical advances in public health, which have eradicated the threat of such communicable diseases, have also eliminated this check on the rise in homework. Today the homework system poses health risks to the homeworkers and their families. However, public concern has been quite limited in this regard.

Working at home is hazardous to workers' health. Sometimes the hazardous conditions are caused directly by the materials used in the manufacture of garments. In this respect, homeworkers are exposed to risks similar to those faced by workers in garment factories. Inhalation of dust from the fabric is one such risk. One homeworker reports that she had to stop work manufacturing uniforms because she could not tolerate the fabric dust.

> I worked for one firm for nine years, sewing uniforms. I had worked at their factory for a year. Then, after my child was born, I arranged to work at home. But I had to stop, because the material was too dusty. It was some sort of polyester fabric, and I guess I just grew allergic to the dust.

Modern garment factories are equipped with ventilation systems to control such dust, but these health and safety features are not available for a home workplace.

Allergic symptoms are a continuing problem for one homeworker with five years' experience sewing bathrobes at home. She suffers from itching of the nose and throat whenever she works with material that sheds a large quantity of lint.

> The most difficult fabrics are the velours. The nap comes off, and gets all over everything in the house, and the air is filled with it. The dust from this fabric is very fine —

the consistency of flour. If I am sewing with blue velour fabric, my nose begins to run blue. My doctor says it's no good for me to sew this material, even though I am taking allergy shots, but I need the money. Now I usually tie a handkerchief mask over my nose and mouth when I am sewing with velours.

The use of the home as a workplace also means that other family members are exposed to health and safety risks.

Brenda Wong is a mother of two children, one six, the other, sixteen months. Brenda began sewing at home after the birth of her second child. When she started sewing she worked at a table in the basement of the family's modest, two-storey, semi-detached house. Working in the basement had several disadvantages. During the winter months it was cold, too cold, Brenda felt, for the baby. The baby stayed upstairs. The result was that Brenda spent her workday constantly running up and down the stairs to check on the baby. As the baby approached his first birthday and began walking, Brenda tried to persuade her husband to let her move her work area to the living room on the first floor. He objected, first, because it would be unsightly and would detract from the appearance of the home's living room. His second objection was that the sewing produced dust and lint, and a first-floor location would spread the lint throughout the house.

Brenda Wong reports that, after several months of arguing, her husband finally agreed to let her move her work up to the living room. She notes sadly that it wasn't a good solution.

I probably should have listened to him. He was right about the dust from the sewing. Once the machine was upstairs, the dust got all around, and the older child developed allergies to the dust. His eyes got red and itchy, and he was constantly sniffling. The doctor has put him on antihistamines.

Back problems from sitting and sewing for long hours without breaks constitute an additional health problem that afflicts homeworkers. This, too, is comparable to health problems faced by garment workers inside the factories, yet homeworkers have no coverage under worker's compensation.

These ill effects of industrial homework are not unique to the Canadian homeworker labour force. A 1979 survey of conditions of employment among homeworkers in London, England, disclosed some of the same inconveniences. In particular, the English homeworkers cited such hazards as abnormally large quantities of dust or fluff in the air and excessive noise from industrial sewing machines.[5]

STRESS

Probably the major health problem faced by homeworkers is stress. Severe stress often results from the intense pressure of working to meet quotas and deadlines during rush season. In addition, workers are penalized if they make errors.

Another major source of stress is the competing pressure of the two jobs of homemaker and homeworker. Virtually all of the homeworkers acknowledge that working at home means that their work is never done. When asked to identify the disadvantages of homework, the most frequently cited problem was that the workers never felt able to relax. Because there are no fixed hours and no breaks, homeworkers feel that they are under constant pressure to produce.

Children and spouse often resent the time spent on sewing, and expect the women to meet their household responsibilities. Frequently, too, cultural traditions exclude husbands and male children from participating in household chores. This dual burden of work and family responsibilities is a physical and an emotional drain. According to one worker: "Homework is mentally bad. When you have homework, it is always in your head."

A homeworker with many years' experience juggling parenting, housekeeping and sewing responsibilities describes a younger cousin's failure to cope with these demands:

My cousin's children were still very young — two and four. Her doctor finally ordered her to stop sewing at home because it was causing too much stress for her, and her stomach suffered. She would try to do everything. She would jump up from the machine, feed the baby, quick sew in a zipper, stir the pot on the stove, rush back to her machine, rush back to change the baby and keep on sewing. She would eat her own sandwich while she kept sewing. The doctor told her she would get an ulcer if she kept it up. He said that if you work in a factory you only do one thing at a time — and you take time *off* to eat your lunch.

Some homeworkers, older women who have been confined to their homes for many years, have difficulty coping with the outside work world after they have fulfilled their child-rearing responsibilities. The following account by a homeworker in her fifties illustrates how the long years of isolation have rendered her incapable of re-entering the world outside her own home.

I began as a homeworker 20 years ago, when my daughter was only one and a half years old. I had a tenant who asked if I'd mind if she did some home sewing in her room. I needed money as well, and I knew how to sew, so I asked her to get me work. Back then I did blouses. We usually got $1.25 a dozen blouses. Two or three dollars a dozen was then considered very good money.

While my daughter was growing up I continued with the homework. I moved from blouses to dresses. At first I could complete maybe five dresses in a day. Now I am fast, I can do more than ten a day. I generally get $2.50 a dress now.

Recently, I thought I would try working in a factory, as I had done before my daughter was born. I liked the idea of a job you could do all day, then leave behind to go home. When you are a homeworker, you always have work to do. Several months ago, I tried factory work, but I couldn't stand it — I'm just not used to it any more — and had to quit after one week. I hated the streetcar, the buses — they were just so crowded. The people just aren't friendly anymore.

The factory was on piecework, and the others were jealous of a fast worker. They wouldn't talk to me. And then, the supervisor made me repeat a job twice. I was making skirts. First, she had me re-do the hanger loops on the inside of the skirts because she said they were in the wrong position. Then, she had me sew them again, because she said I'd done them the wrong size. I couldn't stand it.

A final disadvantage of the homeworker's situation is that she has no paid sick leave. If she wants to earn money, she must keep on working. This means that many homeworkers continue to do their sewing even when they are ill. According to one woman with four years of experience sewing dresses at home:

If you are really sick and don't work, you just don't get paid. Sometimes, you push yourself to work when you are sick, just so you don't lose the pay.

In summary, the working conditions of many of Canada's homeworkers are archaic and illegal under existing employment standards legislation. Rates of pay are set by the piece, at rates so low that many workers cannot even earn the minimum wage. The work is characterized by seasonal fluctuations, ranging from rush periods with ten to 12-hour days for up to six or even seven days per week, down to slack periods with no work at all. For most homeworkers, the slack periods can total several months in a year. Homeworkers must use industrial sewing machines and other costly industrial equipment, and the great majority of homeworkers are forced to purchase their own machinery. In addition, homeworkers are responsible for servicing and maintenance of the equipment and for the purchase of sewing machine attachments and, on occasion, sewing supplies and notions. Transportation of goods to and from the factory is also, in most cases, the responsibility of the homeworkers.

The homeworker's combined use of her home as family residence and workplace poses severe difficulties for both spheres of activity. Dust, lint, noise and other by-products of the industrial sewing pose health hazards for her and her family, and serve to make the home less attractive and livable. As a workplace, the facilities available in a home — usually a dark, cold basement — are far below the standard provided in most factories. From the worker's viewpoint the home workplace thus represents an unhappy compromise.

Many homeworkers see the injustice of their situation. Some have made attempts to protect themselves from employers' exploitative practices. Homeworkers may keep written records documenting the details of particular styles in order to determine whether piece rates paid are in proportion to the complexity of the styles they have sewn. They may threaten to spoil the work if not kept supplied with sufficient sewing supplies. They may try to locate other homeworkers who are sewing for the same employer, in order to compare piece rates paid for particular types of work. They may talk about quitting or about refusing to do particularly difficult and time-consuming styles.

While such efforts may give individual workers the sense that they are exerting some control over their conditions of employment, they really have no such power. The isolation of this workforce of women hidden away in their own basements guarantees the ineffectiveness of their individual actions. As one homeworker puts it, "Before I can even complain to the boss, I have to get him to come to the phone!"

4 Double Burden and Double Bind

A system that allows a woman to work for wages and fulfill a traditional family role at the same time holds a great deal of appeal. The industrial homeworker can be seen to embody the traditional woman: she cares for her children and runs the household while being a productive member of the economy. In a world of rapidly changing expectations about women's work and family roles, of fast-food outlets and escalating female labour force participation, homeworkers combine the roles of wage worker and houseworker — what may seem from the outside to be an enviable position.

Closer examination reveals a very different picture — one of women forced into unhappy compromises in their roles as paid workers and as mothers and housewives. Obliged to remain at home in order to take care of their children, they spend long hours trying to earn a living at low piecework rates. These women want to devote their attention to their children. Yet interruptions from children reduce the number of articles they can complete in a day's work. Homeworkers continually face the contradiction of being unable to respond to their children's needs because they must keep on sewing. Thus, it is their lack of choices rather than the ideal combination of work and family life that keeps these women in the home. Homeworkers are in fact an unwilling source of cheap labour for Canada's clothing industry.

HOMEWORKERS ARE MOTHERS

When the youngest of her four children was two and a half years old, Denise D'Amico took a job folding sheets in a hospital laundry to help meet family expenses. Five days a week, she took her youngest child to the home of a neighbour — a service that cost her $30 a week. She felt that this arrangement was not good for her son.

"He was just not happy. He cried a lot. He lost weight and kept trying to run back home." Denise and her husband agreed that she should leave her laundry job and try to find a way to work at home and care for the children at the same time. Home sewing seemed to be a solution.

※

Cecilia Montana has three children, aged eleven, nine and five. She has been sewing at home for the past five years, in order to be with her children. Her mother-in-law used to take care of the older children and Cecilia worked in a factory. Cecilia explains that other babysitting alternatives were unsatisfactory.

My husband doesn't trust anyone else with the children — only my mother and my mother-in-law. You can't trust babysitters. You fix food, but the children may not get it. He doesn't want the children going off to someone else's house at seven o'clock in the morning, just so I can get to work in a factory.

※

Frances Chang would consider leaving her three children — aged four, seven and ten — in day care, if she could only find full-day and after-school group day care programs at rates she could afford. Once, several years ago, she got as far as applying for a government subsidy for the children's day care fees, in hopes of getting off homework and moving back into factory work. The plan fell through when she was told she must have a job before the subsidized day care arrangement could begin.

※

Anna Da Silva and her husband have never heard of the system of day care subsidy. Parents of two children, aged two and four, the couple would like to find someone to come in and care for the children in their own home. They would also consider using a day care centre — but they believe that with two children, it would cost more than they could afford. Until the family finds an adequate day care arrangement, Anna will continue home sewing, as she has done for the past year and a half.

The system of day care provision in most urban centres in Canada is such that only the very affluent and the very poorest families have access to licensed day care spaces for their children. Group day care programs are licensed by provincial authorities, and offer full-day care for children of preschool age. Care is provided in a facility called a day care centre. Group day care programs may be run by the government, by commercial operators or by social agencies or private, non-profit and community organizations.

Parent fees for full-time group day care are generally between $50 and $100 a week, or about $3,500 a year. Infant day care centres, caring for children under two years of age, have higher staff-child ratios. In consequence, the fees for infant day care are higher than the fees for other programs.

In Canada, there is provision for the government to pay all or part of the cost of children's day care, through a day care subsidy. A family's eligibility for subsidy is generally determined by criteria of financial need. Subsidy requirements are usually so stringent that only the very poorest families qualify. At present, across Canada, although almost half of the mothers of preschool children are in the labour force, only about 12 per cent of children under six are in licensed day care. The most recent national day care statistics, published by Health and Welfare Canada, indicate that just less than half of the day care spaces in Canada are being subsidized. That leaves the greatest proportion of working parents to try to come up with $75 a week — or more if they have more than one child.

Most of the homeworkers' families are unlikely to receive day care subsidies. They fall into the category of "working poor" — families with total annual incomes in the $15,000 range — and they generally cannot qualify for government assistance. Even if they are eligible, many homeworkers are unaware that subsidy programs are available, because the governments administering the subsidies do not publicize the availability of these monies.

The solution that these families attempt — the simultaneous provision of child care at home and full-time work at industrial sewing — imposes serious stress on the parent-child relationship. Many homeworkers suffer from guilt and worry because they are obliged to neglect their children's needs in order to meet the pressure of rush deadlines for their sewing assignments.

Wendy Tse is a mother of two children, aged one and five. In the year since the birth of her younger child, she has worked at home sewing women's dresses and blouses. Prior to that, she worked for almost four years as a sewing machine operator in a factory. With one child, she was able to use a neighbour as a babysitter. Now that she has a second child, she has been unable to find a suitable babysitting arrangement, so she has decided instead to work at home.

Wendy Tse can find little to recommend homework as a form of employment. "The only one good thing," she says, "is that I can look after the baby." Yet it is clear from her description of the heavy pressures of her daily workload that she has difficulty combining homework and child care.

It is hard, because the sewing has no fixed hours, and there are never any breaks between housework, sewing and child care. I find I get short-tempered with my son when I'm trying to work.

Voula Georgiou sews bathrobes and nightgowns at home while caring for her son who is two and a half years old. A child of that age, she notes, is very active and needs lots of attention. For her part, she must sew at least eight hours a day, and she tries to put in those hours during the day, before her husband returns from work.

While insisting that "My first concern is my child, and then my job," Voula admits that she sometimes has to keep working even when her son is demanding her attention.

Sometimes I just have him sitting up on the sewing machine while I work. Sometimes, though, he sits there saying "No sew." He doesn't want me to do anything, he just wants some attention.

The tragic contradiction in the homeworkers' situation is thus, that although they opt to stay home because of their children, they are unable to give their children the care and attention they need. Discussions with homeworkers reveal the depth of their conviction that a mother's first obligation is to her children. The choice to work in the home represents, in most cases, a sacrifice they are prepared to make on behalf of their children.

Many of the women who had worked in factories, usually in the clothing trades, before their children were born, preferred factory work because it gave them opportunities to meet other adults, form social relationships and be spared the isolation and loneliness of working in their own basements.

Giovanna D'Onofrio, an Italian immigrant, worked as a sewing machine operator in a brassière factory for five years before her children were born. A homeworker for the last three years, she says:

I stay at home just because of the children. Really, I don't suggest to a lot of people to do this kind of thing. You're very busy. It's better to go outside, get out of the house, meet other people.

Annamaria Vecchiarelli is another woman who finds homework extremely isolating, but feels it is necessary while her children are young:

Of course, when my children are older, I would like to work outside my home. It is not healthy to stay inside and never breathe fresh air. I wake up and begin sewing by 7 a.m. I stay inside the house all day. I don't see other people and don't make any friends. In the busy season, I go out once a week for grocery shopping and maybe again on Sunday we go out in the evening to visit relatives or friends.

Similar feelings are expressed by another homeworker, a mother of six:

> What I am doing, I am doing for my kids, not for myself. I work at home so that they can come home for lunch and find me here. Otherwise, I would breathe the fresh air. When you work at home all day you don't meet anyone, you don't know what is going on outside.

Still another homeworker, a 26-year-old Greek immigrant mother of two children, aged 11 months and three years, reports that she would prefer to return to factory work, but for her responsibilities to her children.

> I have been working at home because of the children. I would like to work outside; I feel that I am always closed up here. But it is easier on the children if I don't have to take them out of the house every morning. Also, I am here to cook for them.

HOMEWORKERS ARE HOUSEKEEPERS

In addition to taking care of their children, homeworkers also retain primary responsibility for housekeeping duties. Many women report difficulty fitting a full-time workload of sewing into a day filled with cooking, child care and cleaning chores. There are just not enough hours in the day. Many cope with the problem by beginning work very early in the day, before they cook breakfast for the family. Other hours are fitted in when children are in school, napping or playing alone. Evening gives them more uninterrupted time to sew, although the absence of daylight creates a strain on their eyes. One woman found that she was able to work best if she stayed up a few hours later than the rest of the family. Her husband objected, and she has since agreed not to do any of her sewing after 9 p.m.

Although they work to provide economic necessities for their families, homeworkers often have a hard time justifying to their husbands the hours they spend at the sewing machine. Family responsibilities are rarely lessened just because an additional workload is added.

The following account by an Italian-Canadian woman illustrates how the burden of hours of homework puts a strain on family relationships. Her husband is employed full-time as a janitor, and it is clear that she is uncomfortable about asking him to take on housekeeping duties in the home. At times, however, she has no choice but to enlist his assistance:

> My husband doesn't like it when I have to work at night, to rush an order. When I had the last rush job, I had to work on Saturdays. My husband had to do the grocery shopping and clean the house, and when I went to bed at night, I was totally exhausted. It was too many hours of work in a day for me. My husband complained when I had to work in the evening, but he does understand, if they are coming the next day to pick up an order that I have not yet finished then I will have to work. Sometimes, if I have to work in the evening, then he will do the dishes. Then he feels sorry for me, and I feel sorry for him. He is a good man.

Many of the women report that their families are jealous and resentful of the long hours they spend sewing. Husbands and children alike complain that the women have no free time for recreational activities. The homeworkers' families find the summer months particularly difficult for this reason, since the July and August scheduling of children's school holidays and husbands' vacations coincides with the period of peak demand for labour in the garment industry.

In some cases, husbands do help out with child care so that the women can sew without interruption for long periods of time. Women report that their husbands often find such child care responsibilities burdensome. One typical situation involves a Greek-Canadian family, with two children aged four and ten. The husband drives a truck during the day and the wife sews at home for eight hours each day, six days a week. Like most homeworkers, her sewing hours are intermittent, and are sandwiched between various household chores. She manages to fit in her eight hours of sewing between 6 a.m. and 11 p.m. During the evenings, after dinner, her husband helps to look after the children, but, she says, "he really doesn't like to do that after working all day."

Some women claim that their families make no objection to their long hours of homework. It is clear from most of these women's comments, however, that their families' approval is contingent upon the women fulfilling their household obligations. Says one worker,

My husband has no complaints about my work, everything is ready on time.

In another instance, it is apparent that the husband's support is not unqualified:

When everything in the household is perfect and I'm not miserable, he is satisfied.

Homework is women's employment. It arises when women are forced to do wage labour simultaneously with household labour. Homeworkers are not alone in bearing the double burden of work and family responsibilities. All working mothers face the problem of fulfilling the demands of these two roles. For most women, however, there is a physical separation between their work environment and their family environment. For the homeworker, forced to integrate the two, the problems are exaggerated.

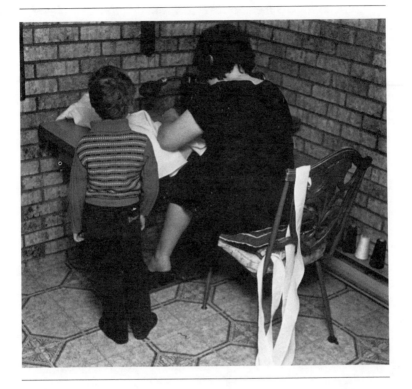

HOMEWORKERS ARE IMMIGRANTS

An additional defining characteristic of homeworkers is that they are workers lacking in alternatives in the labour market. As a group, homeworkers are women who have had little formal education and whose job experience has been limited to sewing in garment factories.

Immigrant mothers of young children frequently have language problems that further limit their employment possibilities. Their daily routine, which ties them to home and children, offers few opportunities to learn English. The addition of a full-time homework workload to their domestic routine serves as further insulation from the English-speaking culture.

The experience of Kim Lee, an immigrant from Hong Kong and mother of two children under five years old, is illustrative of the set of factors that operate to create the homework labour force.

For the past year and a half, Kim Lee has been employed by a women's sportswear company to sew skirts and slacks at home on a piecework basis. She works between seven and nine hours a day, generally for five, six or seven days a week, depending on the amount of work and the pressure of deadlines from the manufacturer.

Kim Lee came to Canada six years ago. For three and a half of those years she worked as a sewing machine operator inside a Toronto garment factory. When her children were younger, she and her husband, a restaurant cook, worked different shifts. Kim cared for the children while he worked during the evenings; he watched the children while she worked during the days. There was a two-hour overlap in their shifts during the afternoon, when they employed an Italian neighbour to babysit. They knew and trusted this neighbour and they could also afford her rates of three dollars per afternoon. This arrangement broke down when the Lee family had to move from their apartment. They found a new place to rent, but have been unable to make a new babysitting arrangement in the year and a half they have lived in a new neighbourhood. Since then, Kim Lee has worked as a homeworker.

Both Kim Lee and her husband would prefer for her to work outside. Her annual homework earnings are $4,000. "I get paid half of what I used to earn in the factory, and it is very unsteady," she explains.

Kim Lee is typical of the majority of women who make up the homework labour force. Their ethnic origins vary — they may come from Italy, Greece, China, Portugal or elsewhere — but they are typically immigrants to Canada. Most lack proficiency in English. Their life routines keep them using their native languages, even though they may have been in Canada for many years. Virtually all homeworkers are married. Depending on ethnicity, their spouses tend to be employed in such industries as construction, food service, transportation and manufacturing. Like Kim Lee, most homeworkers are between the ages of 25 and 40, and most have relatively little formal education.

DECIDING TO BE A HOMEWORKER

The idea of doing homework may be a woman's own — the usual pattern — or it may be suggested by the husband. One woman, married to a cutter in a dress factory, reported that her husband introduced the idea that he could bring home bundles of work for her to sew. Another woman reported that her family was having a particularly hard time meeting expenses. Her husband worked in outside construction, and his work had been limited because of a building slump. She recalls,

He asked me if I would start sewing at home. I was willing to sacrifice for the sake of the family.

While the need to care for young children is by far the most common reason trapping homeworkers in the home, there are additional reasons — generally other family obligations — which also operate to keep women at home. Providing care for an invalid husband keeps one 50-year-old woman working full-time at home to produce hand-knitted sweaters for a Toronto retailer. Another woman in her fifties is helping to keep her son's family intact while the son is serving a prison term. She does home sewing as well as providing child care for her two young grand-children while her daughter-in-law works. There are also some older homeworkers who have physical disabilities or handicaps of their own which make it difficult for them to travel to a factory workplace on a daily basis. Homework enables them to earn badly needed income without leaving their homes.

The great majority of the women who do homework have had experience as inside workers in the needle trades industry. Like Kim Lee, most of them worked out of the home until child care responsibilities made their factory employment impossible. Kim Lee's experience is also typical in that with only one young child, women often find it possible to make acceptable day care arrangements with relatives or neighbours. Such informal arrangements become increasingly more complicated as children grow and as families have more than one child, and it is at this stage that many of the women begin to do homework.

As a system of employment, the homework system is founded on economic need, cheap labour and a lack of available child care services for working parents. The need to care for the young, the physically disabled or the obligation to provide other forms of support to the family in times of difficulty can confine women to the home for years at a time. Few homeworkers consider homework a satisfactory type of employment, and most plan to return to inside factory work when their children grow older. Such, in fact, is the typical work history pattern for these women: they begin their working careers as factory workers; they bring their work home when their children are young; and as their children grow older, they return to the factories. In some instances, as the women grow older, physical disabilities may once again drive them out of the factories back to working at home. The general pattern is the same: the homework system preys upon workers who operate at a disadvantage in the labour market, women whose obligations to their families trap them at home.

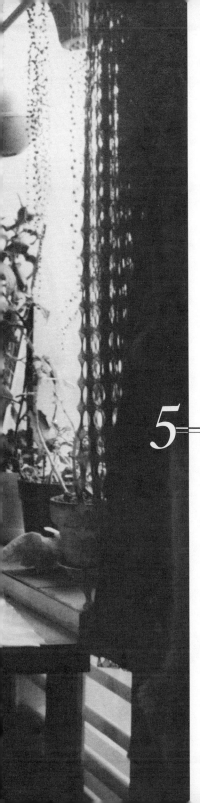

5   The Unprotected Homeworker

*T*he government's role in relation to homework includes employment standards, taxes, workers' benefits and labour relations. Some of these are provincial government responsibilities, others are federal. Throughout the complex of legislation and regulations the Canadian homeworker is set apart from other working people, and in fact receives little protection. A review of the relevant legislation reveals a number of laws, provisions and interpretations that must be changed before homeworkers can be elevated from their second-class status in the labour force.

The employment of homeworkers in Canada is subject to regulation by provincial employment standards legislation. But the combination of a high proportion of employers who ignore requirements for registration of homeworkers and the failure of governments to impose fines or other penalties on employers who are found to violate existing standards means that the practice of homework is, for the most part, unregulated.

The majority of homeworkers in Canada work outside the system of government regulation and control. In Ontario, as in Quebec and other centres of the garment industry across North America, these so-called "illegal homeworkers" far outnumber those covered by government regulations. The commonly-used term "illegal homeworker" is really a misnomer. It is generally the employer and not the homeworker who is in violation of the law — for not reporting the use of homework labour to government authorities. By violating employment standards legislation and, in some cases, collective agreements with unions, manufacturers make big savings on labour costs. Some of the unreported homeworkers are immigrants who are working illegally in Canada, and who accept the substandard wages and working conditions associated with homework in exchange for anomymity.

The existence of illegal homework in Ontario and Quebec is confirmed by a wide variety of sources, including representatives of the industry, provincial government officials and union staff, as well as members of the advisory committees that oversee labour practices in the garment industry. Spokespersons from these sectors provide varying assessments of the number of homeworkers unreported by their employers as a proportion of the total homework labour force. In Toronto, estimates range from 60 per cent to 90 per cent. The numbers are greater in Quebec, but the pattern appears to be the same; most homework is done outside the system of government regulation and control.

In order to evaluate the scope of the problem, it is necessary to have some idea of the real number of home-workers. This can be estimated for the province of Ontario by combining available statistics with a bit of detective work.

One way in which employers recruit homeworkers is through classified advertisements. My co-workers and I selected 30 advertisements for home sewers from Toronto English-language daily newspapers, the *Chinese Express* and several smaller ethnic newspapers. A check was then made to determine which of these 30 manufacturers had permits. Ten were found to be operating with permits; 20 had none.

This 1:2 ratio of legal to illegal homework firms is a conservative estimate of the scale of illegal use of home-workers. Since the source of information was published advertisements, and since firms operating without home-work permits might be reluctant to advertise openly for homeworkers, this sample is almost certainly biased towards firms operating within the law. It is likely that non-permit holders tend to hire their staff using less formal, word-of-mouth methods.

Keeping this in mind, we will still estimate the number of homeworkers in Ontario. In 1980, there were 254 homeworker permits issued for the province. Assuming that the 1:2 ratio of permit-holders to non-permit-holders that exists in the needle trades prevails in other sectors, these 254 are matched by an additional 508, making a total of 762 employers in the province. Within the women's dress and sportswear industry, each homework permit covers an average of ten homeworkers. (Some employers are issued permits for significantly more homeworkers; for example, one manufacturer's permit covers 70 homeworkers.) If homework in other industries operates on the same scale, this would yield a total of 7,620 homeworkers in the province, only 2,540 of whom are covered by official permits.

The Canada Employment and Immigration Commission reported that in 1978, there were 28,000 clothing workers in Ontario. From our estimate, we can then say that homeworkers comprise at least one-quarter of the clothing workers in Ontario. Undoubtedly, this estimate of the proportion of homeworkers to factory workers is also very low.

In both Ontario and Quebec, the laws governing the practice of homework are weak and ineffective. One obstacle to more rigorous imposition and enforcement of standards is the reluctance on the part of policymakers to consider persons who work in their own homes as employees. There is a tendency to look upon workers based in a home setting as artisans, craftspeople or skilled workers who are self-employed. According to this inaccurate and romanticized view, homeworkers are independent workers, responsible for their own working conditions.

A Canadian Broadcasting Corporation radio news program aired on October 28, 1980 provides a good example of this general misconception about the nature of homework. Ostensibly a feature on craftspeople, the program documented the exploitation of women who work as hand knitters, producing sweaters for elite, high fashion boutiques. One interview presented a woman who hand knitted sweaters for a company that employed over 200 home knitters. The woman explained that she produced garments according to patterns supplied by her employer, using materials supplied by him as well. She said she was paid between $12 and $25 each for the sweaters, which then retailed for hundreds of dollars each. The commentator addressed the problem in the context of the difficulties encountered by craftspeople trying to market their work. Yet the number of workers and the fact that each is supplied with patterns and materials shows quite clearly that they are not self-employed craftspeople. The workers who produce garments for knitwear manufacturers — and there is a rapidly growing number working in this high fashion industry — are employees, and should be entitled to the rights that are considered basic for other workers.

In fact, employment standards legislation in both Ontario and Quebec is clear in defining homeworkers as employees. Both provinces also maintain procedures for the regulation and control of homework. Yet in both provinces, the regulatory procedures fail to guarantee the right of individual homeworkers to decent conditions of employment.

ONTARIO REGULATIONS

In the province of Ontario, the only legislation that refers directly to homeworkers is the *Employment Standards Act,* which establishes minimum standards and conditions of employment. Specifically, the *Employment Standards Act* includes under employees: "a person who does homework for an employer." According to the Act, homework is defined to mean:

the doing of any work in the manufacturing, preparation, improvement, repair, alteration, assembly or completion of any article or thing or any part thereof in premises occupied primarily as living accommodation; and "homeworker" has a corresponding meaning.[1]

In practice, the *Employment Standards Act* contains two provisions that affect homeworkers: payment at no less than the minimum wage rate and vacation pay at four per cent of annual earnings. With regard to wages, the Act stipulates that where a homeworker is paid piecework rates, the rates must be high enough to ensure the employee is able to earn at least the minimum wage. The Act also sets out employment standards in a number of other areas, including hours of work, overtime pay, public holidays, maternity leave, benefit plans and termination of employment. Homeworkers, however, are specifically exempted from coverage for the first three, while the other provisions — maternity leave, termination of employment and employer-provided benefit plans — are rarely applicable. Even the provisions concerning minimum wage rates and vacation pay are, unfortunately, rarely enforced.

ONTARIO'S PERMIT SYSTEM

The Act also provides for the regulation of homework through a system of government permits issued to employers. According to the *Employment Standards Act,* no person shall employ a homeworker without a permit issued by the Director of Employment Standards. The Director is empowered to issue or to revoke a permit on such terms as he or she thinks advisable. As mentioned earlier, approximately 250 permits are issued annually in a variety of industries, each covering an average of about ten homeworkers.

The needle trades industries account for about half of all homework permits in the province. The largest user of homework is the women's dress and sportswear industry. Children's wear, blouses and novelty items also account for a large proportion of homework.

The permit system puts the onus on the employer to obtain a permit and to conform to the employment standards regulations. It is the policy of the Ministry to investigate suspected violations by employers only when a formal complaint has been received. This is not a frequent occurrence, however. Homeworkers as a group are not aware of their legal rights, and most of them are neither sufficiently fluent in English nor familiar enough with the bureaucratic system to be able to lodge a complaint against an employer.

Permits are valid for one year, and are issued in December. The permit application requires the employer to list the names and addresses of all prospective homeworkers, as well as to provide a description of the article(s) he or she proposes to have the homeworkers manufacture. Within the garment industry, the employer must describe the style or styles of garments to be assigned to homeworkers, and state the unit cost to be paid for each piece completed, as well as the hourly wage rate that such a piece rate represents.

The one-year duration of these permits gives the system a farcical character. The garment industry is characterized by rapidly changing styles. Changing seasons and changing fashion trends mean that employers alter the styles given out to homeworkers on almost a weekly basis. But the law requires an employer to provide detailed information about the styles and unit costs only once a year. In addition, although employers with permits are supposed to inform Employment Standards on a monthly basis of any changes in the names and addresses of the homeworkers working for them, this provision is not enforced.

Thus, even for the minority of employers who do conform to regulations and apply for and obtain a permit to use homeworkers, that permit is, in effect, a licence to set their own terms. Beyond the annual review of piece rates paid at one particular time in the year (and, where applicable, a monthly payroll audit by an advisory committee), there is no guarantee that even the homeworkers covered by permits will receive the minimum wage as required by law. And, in fact, they do not.

The Ontario homework permit stipulates that an employer must provide the transportation or cover the cost of transportation of goods to the homeworker's home, and must also take responsibility for picking up her completed work. Yet interviews with many of the homeworkers covered by these permits reveal that this provision is not adhered to. Homeworkers themselves incur considerable expense transporting garments to and from the factories. Sometimes their husbands provide this service in the family car; in other cases, the women carry the large bundles of garments by taxi, at considerable personal expense.

Within the women's dress and sportswear industry, some of the government's responsibility for checking up on applicants for homework permits has been delegated unofficially to the Advisory Committee for Ladies' Dress and Sportswear. This five-person advisory committee, established under the terms of the province's *Industrial Standards Act,* consists of two representatives from unions and three from management (including both union and nonunion firms). Members are appointed by the Minister of Labour, and are responsible for establishing wage schedules and supervising employment practices in the industry.

The Advisory Committee is funded by payroll contributions from employers and employees in all Ontario firms within the industry. According to its director, the Advisory Committee is responsible both to the Minister and to the industry. Unlike the Ministry of Labour, which regulates employment standards on a complaint basis, checking alleged violations, the Advisory Committee operates by reviewing monthly payroll records from each firm within the industry. However, for those firms that do not report their homeworkers, only individual complaints are investigated.

When an employer in the ladies' dress and sportswear industry applies for a permit to hire homeworkers, the application is reviewed by the Advisory Committee. It also reviews the piece rates proposed by the employer, to determine whether they would enable a homeworker to earn the minimum wage. Finally, the Advisory Committee makes a recommendation to the Ministry about whether or not the permit should be issued.

In addition to this role as unofficial reviewer of homework permit applications, the Advisory Committee investigates suspected cases of employers using homeworkers without a permit. In such instances, employers are advised of the requirement that they apply for and obtain a permit before utilizing homeworkers. Information about violations of the permit regulations is passed on to the Ministry. Although, as we have seen, homeworkers comprise at least 25 per cent of the clothing workers in Ontario, the supervisor of the Advisory Committee estimates that only between 5 and 10 per cent of the two inspectors' time is spent on homework.

Despite the existence of this official system of permits and regulations, the homework system remains largely unregulated. Part of the reason for this is the poor enforcement of the existing regulations. An additional reason is the contracting system of labour that characterizes the clothing industry. As mentioned in the first chapter, clothing manufacturers frequently contract out the actual sewing of garments to independent contractors. Some contractors have factories, some just use homeworkers, some use a combination of in-factory workers and homeworkers. Many are small, many subcontract the work to still others — which means that the whole system is difficult to scrutinize and regulate. Whether the real number of homeworkers in Ontario is close to 7,620 — or, as is more probable, a figure that is considerably higher, it is clear that homework in Ontario is a subterranean system, operating outside public scrutiny and regulation.

QUEBEC REGULATIONS

The province of Quebec is the centre of the clothing industry in Canada, and has, correspondingly, the largest share of homeworkers. In Quebec, as in Ontario, most homeworkers are unregistered and unreported. An article by Jennifer Robinson in the *Montreal Gazette* ("Kitchen Becomes a Sweatshop," August 30, 1980) estimated that 10,000 Quebec women are part of the "black labour market." The largest number of these are home sewers.

Quebec also has standards and regulations designed to protect the rights of homeworkers and to restrict their numbers. Homework in Quebec is subject to two pieces of legislation. Quebec's equivalent to Ontario's *Industrial Standards Act* is the *Act Respecting Collective Agreement Decrees*. This legislation allows any party to a collective agreement in any industry to apply to the Minister of Labour and Manpower to pass a decree making the collective agreement binding on all employers and employees in that industry. Each decree is administered by a joint committee.

Decrees have been established in numerous sectors of the apparel trades in Quebec, including ladies' dress, ladies' cloak and suit, boys' clothing and the glove industry. These decrees deal specifically with homework, and each of them in the various sectors deals differently with the issue.

Homework is permitted by the decrees controlling the women's garment industries. The decree relating to the dress industry (Decree No. 3519) defines homework as "the manufacture of garments done in or about a home or residence" and prohibits it only for shop employees already employed by a firm governed by the decree. The decree includes instructions for the calculation of piece rates to homeworkers, specifying that those rates must exceed by ten per cent the rates paid inside the factory. This differential is intended to cover homeworkers' costs for equipment and utilities. The decree also specifies that the employer must pay the homeworker for the work at the time he or she picks up the goods; that the employer must supply all thread and be responsible for all transportation of goods. Finally, the employer cannot charge the homeworker for the cost of using someone else to re-do any work not done to the employer's satisfaction.

Homework is prohibited in Quebec's men's and boys' clothing industry (Decree No. 711) and is restricted to a small fraction of total production in the province's leather glove industry.

Quebec's homeworkers are also subject to the protection of the province's *Labour Standards Act,* which covers minimum labour standards for the province. According to this Act, homeworkers are entitled to receive the minimum wage.

TAXES AND BENEFITS

For the Canadian government, the issue of homeworkers' tax obligations and entitlement to unemployment insurance and Canada Pension benefits hinges on whether the homeworker is considered to be an employee or a contractor. Homeworkers are not specifically mentioned in any of the provisions of the Unemployment Insurance Commission, Canada Pension Plan or the *Income Tax Act*.

The question of homeworkers' tax status seems particularly unclear. Conversations with a variety of persons in the field, including provincial government staff, some employers and homeworkers themselves, reveal a widespread belief that homeworkers are entitled to business deductions for Canadian income tax purposes. If this were so, homeworkers could claim deductions for machinery and transportation costs as well as for the expenses involved in using their own household space and utilities. This interpretation, however, is vehemently denied by a spokesperson from the Rulings Division of the Revenue Canada office, who explains that the question of homeworker status is handled on an individual case-by-case basis. The same procedure is relevant for unemployment insurance and Canada Pension Plan benefits, for these also fall under the jurisdiction of Revenue Canada. A ruling on a homeworker's entitlement to unemployment insurance compensation or pension plan benefits will likely be accepted for all three purposes. (It is possible that some homeworkers do claim business deductions in their income tax returns without first obtaining a formal ruling. Revenue Canada does not compel employers or homeworkers to request such a ruling — nor does it make a ruling on every homeworker tax return. The fact remains that there is no official Revenue Canada interpretation of the status of homework.)

While there are tax benefits associated with a homeworker's classification as a contractor, her eligibility for unemployment insurance and responsibility for contributing to Canada Pension Plan depend upon her being considered an employee. In order to determine whether a homeworker is entitled to have unemployment insurance,

Canada Pension or income tax deductions taken from her wages, either the manufacturer or the homeworker herself may apply for a ruling on the matter.

Once an application for such a ruling has been made, an assessor makes a ruling that is legally binding. The main question at issue is the degree of control exercised by the employer. A homeworker is likely to be considered an employee if the manufacturer has hired *her* specifically to do the job; if the manufacturer maintains a high degree of control over the work situation (determines hours of work, imposes deadlines); and if the manufacturer owns the machinery and equipment, all materials involved in the production of the garments, and picks up and delivers the goods. According to a Revenue Canada spokesperson, a homeworker who used to work in a factory and now works at home for the same manufacturer is considered to be an employee because in this case, the home is deemed to be an extension of the workplace.

If, on the other hand, there is more of a contractor relationship between manufacturer and homeworker, the homeworker may be considered self-employed and be able to claim deductions for business expenses. This classification would be applicable if she delegates work to other homeworkers, if she owns her own sewing machine and furnishes thread and lining materials, if there is no supervision provided by the manufacturer, and if she works for a number of different manufacturers. As a contractor, a homeworker is ineligible for unemployment insurance benefits.

If a homeworker is found to be an employee, then pension and unemployment insurance premiums are deducted from her wages and she is covered by both. Income tax is also deducted from the source. On filing her income tax return, she is entitled to claim an expense deduction of only three per cent of her total wages (up to a maximum of $500). If her expenses exceed $500, she can ask her employer to fill out a special form (T-2200) that will be reviewed by Revenue Canada to decide whether she may claim additional expense deductions.

When we examine the terms of employment of homeworkers, the types of expenses they must incur and the job insecurity that characterizes their work, it is clear that the tax laws operate unfairly and to their disadvantage. For the vast majority of homeworkers, the home is actually an extension of the workplace. The worker who operates as a home-based contractor, farming out work to subcontractors and taking on assignments from a number of different manufacturers, is simply not the norm. The fact that homeworkers often own their own machinery and equipment does not prove that they operate as independent contractors; it simply demonstrates that the exploitative homework system enables employers to shift the cost of machinery onto the workers. If homeworkers work for several employers, it is generally because they are not getting enough work from one. In fact, this illustrates that one of the clearest needs of homeworkers is for unemployment insurance, which will provide them with some income during the slow months in the garment industry.

Overall, it is clearly more advantageous for a homeworker to be adjudged an employee than self-employed. As self-employed, she can deduct business expenses against income, but considering how low homeworkers' incomes are, this is scarcely an advantage.

WORK-RELATED INJURY

According to the *Workmen's Compensation Act* of the province of Ontario, a homeworker is defined as an "outworker," and is specifically excluded from the definition of "employee." An outworker is defined as follows in the Act:

> "outworker" means a person to whom articles or materials are given out to be made up, cleaned, washed, altered, ornamented, finished, repaired or adapted for sale in his own home or in other premises not under the control or management of the person who gave out the articles or materials. . .[2]

According to a spokesperson from the Workmen's Compensation Board, the primary reason for excluding homeworkers is because it is difficult to calculate their hours and amount of work, which are the basis for determining compensation. It is also difficult, according to the spokesperson, to demonstrate that a homeworker's injury is incurred "on the job."

The spokesperson explained that homeworkers are termed "subcontractors" for workmen's compensation purposes. He added that homeworkers can work whenever they want, and have no fixed work schedule or specific number of hours they must put in each day. He suggested that homeworkers could meet their insurance needs by getting private individual or group insurance coverage, though he acknowledged that such an option might be unrealistic.

Clearly, homeworkers lack sufficient funds to finance such insurance plans on their own. Yet it is equally clear that their work exposes them to health and safety risks, and that they should be eligible for the worker's compensation plan that is administered by the province.

The issue of the employment status of the homeworker is a problem inherent in the institution of homework. That it is not a uniquely Canadian or even North American problem is clear from an international review of the contract labour system in the clothing industry recently conducted by the International Labour Organization (ILO) in Geneva, Switzerland. Examination of the employment situation of home sewers in many countries indicates that homeworkers are very frequently considered as independent workers or contractors, and are therefore ineligible for labour standards protection or employee benefit plans or other government programs.

The ILO report offers the following comment on the employment status typically accorded to homeworkers:

> It appears anomalous to consider as independent or self-employed a worker who is entirely dependent on work given out to him by a manufacturer or a subcontractor, to be carried out according to the specifications of the latter and paid at rates fixed by him, the more so

since in many cases such workers are using machinery lent or rented to them by the employer and, in almost every case, materials supplied by him.[3]

During the twentieth century, most Canadian working people have achieved basic protection of fair labour practices. Through legislation and regulations at the provincial and federal levels, most workers are guaranteed minimum wage rates; overtime pay for overtime work; paid holidays; a ban on child labour; unemployment insurance and pension benefits; and some protection against health and safety hazards in the workplace.

As a group, homeworkers are denied such protection. The complex of legislation affecting homeworkers operates to their detriment, depriving them of the basic rights guaranteed to other workers. The existing laws and regulations of various levels of government trap homeworkers in a Catch-22 situation. The terms of employment for homeworkers dictated by one level of government are used by another level of government to deprive the homeworker of employee status. Until homeworkers are accorded full employment standards protection and the same benefits available to other workers, they will continue to be the most exploited group of workers in the labour force.

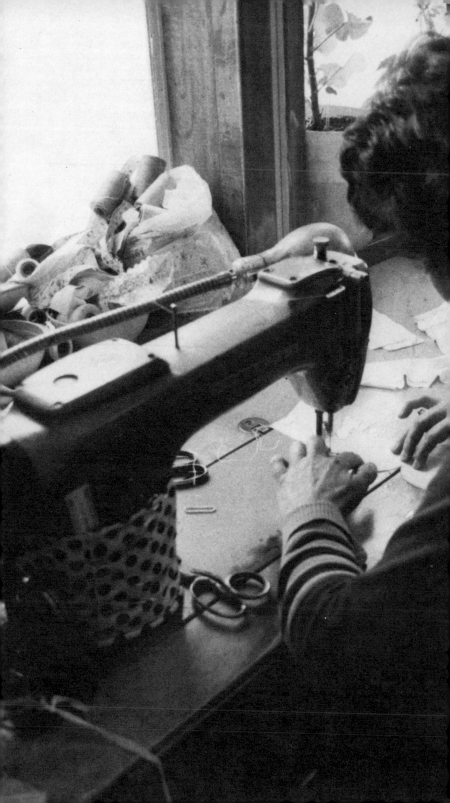

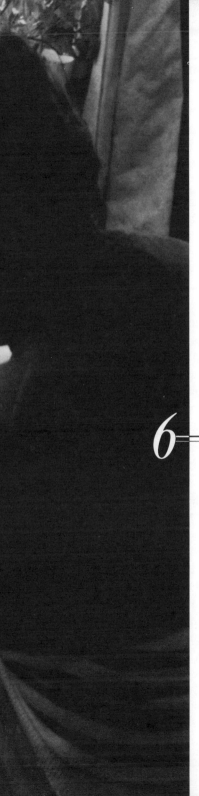

6 THE FUTURE OF HOMEWORK

*H*omeworkers in Canada today are receiving lower wages and working under worse conditions than the rest of the labour force. Can this system be reformed and made more humane? Should workers, unions and government agencies concentrate on eliminating the worst abuses or should they work to abolish homework altogether? A survey of homework past and present has shown that the homeworkers' second-class status is no accident. The abuses discussed in the preceding chapters are an integral part of the system and will disappear only when the system itself is eliminated.

For homeworkers, the primary motive for working at home is a need to juggle family responsibilities with responsibilities for supplementing the family income. But, as it turns out, it is a very unsatisfactory solution. Advocates of the homework system of production argue that making legal provision for homework increases the range of choices for families. On the contrary, the very existence of the homework system reduces the options of working women and their families. This archaic system of production serves to keep wages down, to minimize pressure for publicly-supported child care services and to keep women isolated in their individual households.

For employers, the main incentive for using homeworkers is to save on labour costs. In theory, it would be feasible for governments to draft legislation to guarantee that homeworkers enjoy the same rights and privileges as other workers. Such legislation would have to set their rates of pay higher than those prevailing inside the factories, in order to ensure wage parity plus compensation for the added costs of purchasing and maintaining equipment, utilities and maintenance of the home workspace. Such legislation would have to require that employers assume total responsibility for pick-up and delivery of materials. Such legislation would further have to grant homeworkers the status of employees, thereby according them statutory holidays, unemployment insurance benefits, protection from arbitrary dismissal, notice of layoff and overtime pay. In addition, homeworkers would need to become eligible for union membership, included in a bargaining unit along with inside factory workers.

Given these requirements, the practice of homework would no longer be so profitable for employers. Without that incentive, why would any employer bother to use homeworkers? Not, certainly, out of a sense of social obligation or concern for the welfare of the women who operate the sewing machines — or for their children. As one Toronto sportswear manufacturer put it, "We never told them to have those children."

Under the homework system, supervision and quality control are difficult to maintain, delivery costs are high and the use of a geographically dispersed labour force makes it difficult to meet the production deadlines so important for an industry based on changes in fashion, style and season. In short, if homeworkers were guaranteed equivalent status with other employees, the homework job opportunities would dry up overnight.

Although regulation of homework employment practices is possible in theory, in practice, it is not feasible. For the women working alone in their own basements, there is no way to ensure fair employment practices. It is not by chance that the homework labour force is comprised mainly of isolated, immigrant women with young children. This is a vulnerable population that would be unlikely to stand up for its own rights, even with the protection of additional employment standards legislation. It is not realistic to expect a system of enforcement sufficiently rigorous to ensure protection of the rights of each homeworker.

Advocates of a system of legalized homework maintain that official recognition of homework makes it possible to set standards for wage rates, employee benefits and health and safety regulations — and permits enforcement of such standards. This argument was used in the United States in 1981, when an official of the Reagan administration testified before a congressional committee on labour standards. Raymond Collyer, Deputy Under Secretary of Labor, suggested that the 40-year-old ban on homework had not eliminated the practice, but had merely driven it underground:

> What is the real effect of the current regulations? If a homeworker in a restricted industry does not receive the minimum wage and files a complaint, the remedy provided by the regulations is to deny the complainant further employment, not to assure payment of the minimum wage. Because of this, a homeworker has a choice — get less than the minimum wage or nothing. The choice is no real choice at all.[1]

The experience of Toronto homeworkers and their Montreal counterparts indicates that this argument is false. The existence of a set of standards and regulations provides no guarantee that individual homeworkers will be treated according to those standards. Lax enforcement renders the regulations virtually worthless, and the fact that government and advisory committee staff spend only a small percentage of their time dealing with homework ensures lax enforcement of the regulations. Even where an individual homeworker demonstrates the initiative and the language skills necessary to make a formal complaint about unfair labour practices to the government bureaucracy, she is unlikely to have a successful resolution of her complaint. The employer has all the advantages — the individual homeworker has none.

In April, 1980, the province of Quebec implemented a new employment standards act, which ostensibly guarantees homeworkers the same basic protection as most other employees. The Act is supposed to ensure that all homeworkers are paid the current minimum hourly wage of $3.65 (or equivalent in piece rates) and that they receive paid vacation, holidays and maternity leave. However, according to Pierre Marois, Quebec's social development minister, the legislation fails to protect the thousands of homeworkers whose employers do not obtain permits. Quoted in the *Montreal Gazette* on August 30, 1980, Marois said, "We have to find a way to enforce the law." The Quebec system of enforcement is based on a worker filing a complaint to report any violation of the regulations. The same article quoted Jean-Marc Beliveau, president of the government's Work Standards Commission, "We've been waiting since April for complaints from homeworkers who are exploited."

There has been ample experience with systems of regulation that depend on workers' complaints to know that these methods do not work. When the onus is on the employee to report violations, the violations do not get reported, and standards and regulations are not enforced.

The proposal to ban homework has been made before. In 1964 in Geneva, the International Labour Organization (ILO) convened the First Tripartite Technical Meeting for the Clothing Industry to examine problems affecting workers employed under various subcontracting arrangements, including homework. At that meeting, the following resolution was passed:

> Industrial homework in the clothing industry should, as a matter of principle, ultimately be abolished, except as to certain individuals, for example physically handicapped persons — who cannot adapt themselves to factory work.[2]

While the ILO report thus advocated the abolition of homework in the long term, in the short term it pressed for strict regulation of homework, as specified in the following resolution:

> Where it is not yet practicable to eliminate homework from the clothing industry, governmental regulations — including registration of homeworkers, agents and employers — should be strictly applied in an attempt to

ensure that labour conditions and social security standards of industrial homeworkers are to the maximum
possible extent identical with those of the factory
workers.[3]

The fight against the injustices of the homework system in Canada cannot be won without strong leadership
by the clothing workers' unions. Rivalry between various
unions, loss of jobs through Third World imports and concern about the depressed state of the Canadian clothing
industry have consumed union resources. In the mean-
time, many workers in the industry continue to labour
under archaic conditions of employment. The clothing
unions must do more than pass resolutions condemning
the practice of homework — they must lead the fight to
eliminate the homework system.

In the long term, the home manufacture of clothing
may eventually be eliminated through the modernization
of the industry. At present, the industry is still very
labour-intensive. As the Canadian clothing industry
adopts more modern production techniques, it will
become increasingly less advantageous for manufacturers
to use homeworkers. There is a trend towards larger factories, combined with a movement towards a unit system
of garment making, an increased division of labour in
which individual operators produce only one small section
or component of the garment.

A 1978 report by the Consultative Task Force on the
Canadian Textile and Clothing Industries observes that
while "the principal production activity within the apparel
industry has been and will continue to be sewing, . . . the
operating fact is that, on average, 80% of the production
worker's time is spent taking work to and from the needle;
with only 20% actual sewing."[4] Manufacturers are striv-
ing to improve that ratio by decreasing the number of different operations each worker performs. Thus, instead of

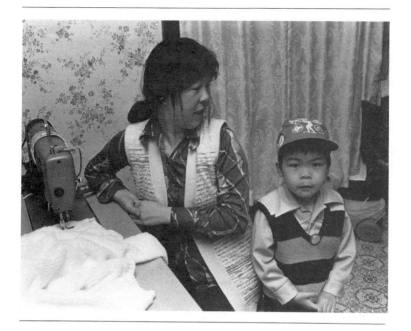

producing an entire garment, or even an entire sleeve, an operator in a modern plant may be responsible only for sewing a piece of trim onto a cuff. In addition to speeding up the rate of production, this eliminates the demand for skilled seamstresses capable of producing an entire garment. In the words of one Toronto sportswear manufacturer, "Technology, not altruism, will wipe out homework in Canada."

While the long-term goal must be the elimination of homework, the short-term goal must be to improve the capacity for enforcement of controls and regulations on the use of homework. There need to be more "teeth" in the regulations that do exist. The existing system for government regulation of homework works to the advantage of the employer and the disadvantage of the homeworker. There is little incentive for an employer to abide by the regulations and little disincentive to cheat.

During the past year, the Employment Standards Branch of the Ontario Ministry of Labour audited the employment practices of a sample of homework permit holders. When asked about the results of that confidential investigation, the Minister of Labour reported that some employer violations were found, but that these appeared to result from employers' "misunderstandings" of the homeworker provisions of the law. This is certainly a casual approach to enforcement. Ignorance of the law is not allowable in other areas. Try telling the police when they pull you over on the highway that you didn't know the speed limit!

One way to strengthen the laws pertaining to homework is to raise the level of fines for violations. At the same time, it is essential to increase the capacity for government and advisory committee inspectors to monitor homeworkers' employment conditions. It takes a considerable allocation of time and effort to achieve this goal, and to do it would require an increase in the amount of staff time devoted to such monitoring. At the very least, the government should undertake a comprehensive investigation into the current working conditions of homeworkers, including an assessment of the extent of illegal homework. Unlike the results of the Ministry's recent audits of homework employers, the findings of such a review must be made available to the general public.

Since isolation contributes to homeworkers' powerlessness to improve their working conditions, steps should be taken to facilitate communication between them. Employers should be required to keep up-to-date records of all homeworkers in their employ, and to make their names, addresses and telephone numbers available to each of their homework employees.

A more ambitious approach to the elimination of the abuses of the homework system is to alter the conditions that lead women to accept this exploitative form of employment. It is evident that the lack of child care is the chief barrier keeping homeworkers out of the regular labour force. If these women had access to high quality, affordable child care, few of them would choose to remain in their basements, combining industrial sewing with their child care and family responsibilities and enlisting the labour of their children to help meet their production quotas. An increase in the supply of such child care service would go a long way toward solving the problem of homework in Canada.

Quality, neighbourhood-based day care would permit many homeworkers to work outside of the home. Workplace day care is another option. It has long been recognized that day care is a pressing need among women in the garment industry. In the United States, the Amalgamated Clothing and Textile Workers' Union runs six child care centres. The programs are funded jointly through contributions by employers and union. In Winnipeg, Manitoba, a workplace day care centre is operating with joint funding by the provincial government and a clothing manufacturer. This pilot program at the Great West Garments (GWG) Limited factory was opened in fall 1980. Such initiatives as these can help to alleviate the practice of homework.

The existence of homework in Canada in the 1980s is a source of shame and embarrassment to the levels of government responsible for maintaining employment standards, and to the trade unions in Canada's clothing industry. It also provides an unfair competitive edge for those apparel producers who utilize subminimum wage labour and ignore employment standards provisions relating to homework. For the homeworkers themselves, trapped in their basement sweatshops, working long hours of the day and night for starvation wages, homework is the only option for earning needed money while caring for their children. Whether by expansion of quality child care services, provision of increased maternity and child care allowances, increasing employment opportunities, or through improvement of language and job training opportunities, these women must be offered alternatives to homework.

FOOTNOTES

1 THE HIGH PRICE OF FASHION

1. Canada, Industry, Trade and Commerce, *Report of the Consultative Task Force on Textiles and Clothing* (Montreal, 1978), pp. 1-2.
2. GATT-fly, *The Textile and Clothing Industries in Canada: A Profile* (Toronto, 1980), p. 14.
3. Sheila McLeod Arnopoulos, *Problems of Immigrant Women in the Canadian Labour Force* (Canadian Advisory Council on the Status of Women, 1979), p. 7.
4. See, for example: Debbie Parkes, "3 Back-Breaking Weeks in the Spadina Sweatshops" (*Toronto Star*, December 29, 1980) and Sheila Arnopoulos' series on "Exploitation of Immigrant Women in Montreal's Garment Industry" (The *Montreal Star*, March/April, 1974).
5. Canada, Textile and Clothing Board, *Textile and Clothing Inquiry*, Vol. 1 (1980), pp. 60, 62.

2 THE ORIGINS OF INDUSTRIAL HOMEWORK

1. "Report on the Sweating System in Canada," *Sessional Papers*, Vol. II, No. 61 (1896), p. 23.
2. E.P. Thompson, *The Making of the English Working Class* (Middlesex, England: Penguin Books, 1968), p. 313, quoting a contemporary description of Cleckheaton, England, in the 1830s.
3. *Daily Mail and Empire* (Toronto, October 9, 1897), p. 10.
4. Clementina Black, ed., *Married Women's Work* (London, 1915), p. 171.
5. "Sweating System in Canada," p. 11.
6. *Daily Mail and Empire*, p. 10.
7. Caroline Manning, *The Immigrant Woman and Her Job* (Washington, D.C., 1930), p. 142.
8. Elizabeth Beardsley Butler, *Women and the Trades: Pittsburgh, 1907-1908* (New York, 1911), p. 137.

9. Manning, *The Immigrant Woman,* p. 147.

10. Butler, *Women and the Trades,* p. 138.

11. "Sweating System in Canada," p. 10.

12. Manning, *The Immigrant Woman,* p. 154.

13. New York State Department of Labor, Bulletin No. 199, as quoted in Lazare Tepper and Nathan Weisberg, "Aspects of Industrial Homework in Apparel Trades" (New York, 1941), p. 18.

14. "Sweating System in Canada," p. 21.

15. Manning, *The Immigrant Woman,* pp. 138-139.

16. Tepper and Weinberg, "Industrial Homework," p. 30.

17. Frieda S. Miller, "Industrial Homework in the United States," *International Labour Review,* Vol. XLIII (January 1941), p. 1.

18. Rinker Buck, "The New Sweatshops," *New York Magazine* (January 29, 1979), p. 40; *Toronto Star* (May 5, 1981), p. 24.

19. Bureau of National Affairs, *Daily Labor Report* (Washington, D.C., May 19, 1981), p. F6.

3 A CAPTIVE LABOUR FORCE

1. British Columbia Ministry of Labour, "Manpower Analysis of the Garment Industry" (1974).

2. Sheila McLeod Arnopoulos, *Problems of Immigrant Women in the Canadian Labour Force* (Canadian Advisory Council on the Status of Women, 1979).

3. Louise Lamphere, "Fighting the Piece-rate System," *Case Studies on the Labor Process,* Andrew Zimbalist, ed. (New York: Monthly Review Press, 1979), p. 267.

4. Joint Commission for the Dress Industry of the Province of Quebec, personal communication, 1979.

5. This is one of the terms and conditions that appear on the Ontario Ministry of Labour "Permit to Employ Homeworkers" under the *Employment Standards Act.* See Chapter Five for a more thorough discussion of this.

6. Simon Crane, *The Hidden Army,* Pamphlet No. 11 (London: Low Pay Unit, 1979).

5 THE UNPROTECTED HOMEWORKER

1. Ontario, *The Employment Standards Act* (Queen's Printer for Ontario, 1976), s.1(c)(ii) and s.1(g).
2. Ontario, *Workmen's Compensation Act* (Queen's Printer for Ontario, 1970), s. 1(l)(ha) and s.1(1)(t).
3. International Labour Organization, *Contract Labour in the Clothing Industry,* Report II, Second Tripartite Technical Meeting for the Clothing Industry (Geneva, 1980), p. 45.

6 THE FUTURE OF HOMEWORK

1. Bureau of National Affairs, *Daily Labor Report* (Washington, D.C., May 19, 1981).
2. Tripartite Technical Meeting for the Clothing Industry, Geneva, 1964, International Labour Organization, *Contract Labour in the Clothing Industry,* Report II, Second Tripartite Technical Meeting for the Clothing Industry (Geneva, 1980), p. 1.
3. Ibid.
4. Canada, Industry, Trade and Commerce, *Report of the Consultative Task Force on Textiles and Clothing* (Montreal, 1978), p. 7.

BIBLIOGRAPHY

Arnopoulos, Sheila. "Exploitation of Immigrant Women in Montreal's Garment Industry." *Montreal Star,* March/April, 1974.

Arnopoulos, Sheila. *Problems of Immigrant Women in the Canadian Labour Force.* Canadian Advisory Council on the Status of Women, 1979, p. 7.

Black, Clementina, ed. *Married Women's Work* (London, 1915).

British Columbia Ministry of Labour. "Manpower Analysis of the Garment Industry." 1974.

Buck, Rinker. "The New Sweatshops: A Penny for Your Collar." *New York Magazine,* January 29, 1979, pp. 40-46.

Canada, Industry, Trade and Commerce. *Report of the Consultative Task Force on Textiles and Clothing.* Montreal, 1978.

Canada, Textile and Clothing Board. *Textile and Clothing Inquiry.* Vol. 1 (1980).

Centre for Urban Research and Action. *Outwork: An Alternative Mode of Employment.* Melbourne, Australia: CURA, 1978.

Cragg, Arnold and Tim Dawson. *Qualitative Research Among Homeworkers,* Research Paper No. 21. London: Department of Employment, 1981.

Crine, Simon. *The Hidden Army,* Pamphlet No. 11. London: Low Pay Unit, 1979.

GATT-fly. *The Textile and Clothing Industries in Canada: A Profile.* Toronto, 1980.

Hakim, Catherine. "Homeworking: Some New Evidence." *Employment Gazette,* Vol. 88, No. 10 (October 1980), pp. 1105-10.

International Labour Organization (ILO). *Contract Labour in the Clothing Industry.* Geneva: ILO, 1980.

International Textile, Garment and Leather Workers' Federation. *Report on Homework.* Brussels: ITGLWF, 1979.

Lamphere, Louise. "Fighting the Piece-rate System." *Case Studies on the Labor Process,* Andrew Zimbalist, ed. New York: Monthly Review Press, 1979.

Lee, Sharon. "Sweatshop." *The Asianadian,* Vol. 3, No. 2 (Fall, 1980), pp. 3-4.

Manning, Caroline. *The Immigrant Women and Her Job.* Washington, D.C., 1930.

Mazur, Jay. "The Return of the Sweatshop." *The New Leader,* August 13, 1979.

McQuaig, Linda. "The Ever-so-Humble and Low Pay at Home." *Macleans,* November 10, 1980.

Ontario Ministry of Culture and Recreation. *Report of Joint Task Force on Immigrant Women,* September 1979.

Thompson, E.P. *The Making of the English Working Class.* Middlesex, England: Penguin Books, 1968.

Trades Union Congress. *Homeworking: A TUC Statement.* London: TUC, 1978.

Wortman, Susan. "The Unhealthy Business of Making Clothes." *Healthsharing,* Vol. 1, No. 1 (November 1979.)

廠 請

ZHTOYNTAI
ZHTOYNTAI πεπειραμένες ράπτριες για
σπίτι από ειδικό κατάστημα φορεμάτων στό
Γιά πληροφορίες τηλεφωνήστε ...τό

WING MACHINE OPERATO
EWORKERS, own indust
hine, LADIES to knit & crochel at home
2 to 6 p.m. needed, call
(15300) 11 a.m.-5 p.m.

OPORTUNIDADES DE TRABAJO

FABRICA DE ZAPATOS
Urgente requiere operadoras
para máquinas de coser para
bajar en casa, excelente
rio llamar al
a viernes
M.
8 A.M. a

EAMSTRESS with strong ma-
ine wanted to start immed. for
rious patching work. Good pay
ould suit single parent or person
anting to work at home. Must be
ick & neat. Interested? Please call

衣廠請人

請內外工多名，長期有貨，銀
King St. W. 一樓
請到：
，五時後電：
或曾. 與麥先生接洽

HAND KNITTING MACHINE
HOMEWORKERS, required.
Must be experienced, have own
machine & be capable of working
from instructions without supervision. Call Mr.
between 4-6.30.

EXPERIENCED home se
with industrial machine for
Coat factory. Apply from 10-12
or 3-5 p.m.

製衣工人

時裝廠請熟手車褲，恤衫，綴等部門
工友 單針，綴骨
另部請剪綫
W.三樓

SEWING Machine Operators &
Sergers for Factory or home work-
ers. Apply in person:
Adelaide St. W.

Sewing Machine Operators for
ABLE to sew full garment
factory or home work.
Richmond St. W.

Sewing Machine Operators

熟
手
時
裝
彩

招 請 製衣

SEWING machine operator
wanted, experienced on piece work
for home sewing. Call 763-1486.
LADIES to knit & crochel al home
needed, call
11 a.m.-5 p.m.

Sewing Machine Operators
CAPABLE of sewing full garment
for factory or home work.
Richmond St. W.

SEWING Machine Operators, ex-
per highest wages in the industry.
permanent inside or outside.
Please call

SEWING machine operators wanted experienced only. Apply
person Rangeview Rd.

最大之皮衣廠請熟
Full-time，薪
Wellin

展 請